Masterpieces

Museum of Fine Arts Budapest

Masterpieces
Museum of Fine Arts Budapest

Edited by
Axel Vécsey
with assistance by Zoltán Bartos

Museum of Fine Arts Budapest 2013

SZÉPMŰVÉSZETI MÚZEUM

Director's Foreword

The building of the Museum of Fine Arts is one of the prime jewels in Heroes' Square, the magnificent square that crowns Budapest's great avenue: this prominent location also serves to indicate the imposing role it has played in Hungary's cultural life. Its creation in 1896 was one of the most significant of the major investments aimed to demonstrate the dynamic development of the country which, on the millennium of its foundation as a state, had moved from being a dominion of Austria to being a partner state of equal rank. The purpose of the new museum was to provide a comprehensive view of the history of the visual arts, thereby also fostering the development of art in Hungary.

What the museum preserves is apparently unchanging, indeed, ideally it should be eternally settled, because the treasures entrusted to us must be passed down without loss from generation to generation. But the very reason we guard the masterpieces so jealously is just because they are not merely the documents of a bygone age. It is our belief that the pinnacles of the history of artistic achievement preserved in the museum convey novel messages to each generation, with relevance to the present day. And as the world changes and always sees something different in the masterpieces, we too have the task of reinterpreting them over and again, of exploring the messages they convey for today.

The small album you are holding gives a taste of the finest pieces in the collections of the Budapest Museum of Fine Arts. From the ocean we have scooped up a few drops of water in which something of the whole is reflected. This volume is a kind of souvenir, and no substitute for perusing the rooms of the museum in person, yet it can help us, later at home, to recollect this world, which (we believe) is immensely rich. It captures the impression of a moment, and inspires us to return at a different moment, with different eyes, discovering new aspects.

Dr. László Baán
Director-General

Introduction

The institution of museums is a characteristic product of nineteenth-century Europe. It is begotten of the idea that the world can and should be perceived, and the path to this cognition is to explore every pebble, every atom of which it is made, to describe them and classify them each in their own suitable category. Once we have classified and arranged the trees, from them emerges the forest: from the great map of their similarities and differences in minute details, their relation to one another, unfolds the general order of the world. The hows and whys of processes of change, and ultimately the driving forces of the universe, manifest themselves. And once we know and understand the world, then in possession of this knowledge we can shape it in our own image. This was an age that desired to construct the new, the modern, not by repealing the past, but as an organic continuation of historical development, as a synthesis of the most excellent of the old achievements; and consequently believed that the key to the creation of great works was the study and understanding of the works of their predecessors – in other words, the museum. And yet there are few large museums in the world that reflect this approach as clearly as the Budapest Museum of Fine Arts. The majority of important public art collections grew out of private collections. And private collectors usually have very different criteria to museums. A private collector has every right to be biased, to purchase pieces that are close to his personal character and taste, that move him.

The basis for many large national collections in the world is given by the treasures of the country's ruling dynasty. Such collections, though not quite as subjective in nature as a private collection, are also born from quite a different motivation to that of a museum. For centuries their function was official representation, in other words to proclaim the greatness, the refined erudition and wealth of the owning dynasty.
Neither private nor dynastic collections were inspired primarily by the thirst for learning, for encyclopaedic knowledge, but rather by the desire to take delight and entertain. But the genesis of the Museum of Fine Arts was different, and this is precisely what gives it its remarkable character. The brief yet fortuitous meeting of an extraordinary moment in history and an extraordinary personality fashioned this cornerstone of Hungarian national culture, and defines its image to this day.

Károly Pulszky inspecting a painting,
1890s
Hungarian National Museum, Historical Photographic Collection

The Museum of Fine Arts is the work of Károly Pulszky (1853–1899). His father Ferenc Pulszky (later director of the Hungarian National Museum) was forced to emigrate after the failed revolution of 1848. His son was born and brought up in London, where he saw how the museums became the supreme symbols of Great Britain's status as a world power and the leaven of national pride. In Pulszky's character a first-class scholar was combined with the boundless ambition of a builder and developer of the nation, who (just like his famed predecessor István Széchenyi with the founding of the Academy of Sciences and other institutions) wanted to raise Hungary to be level with England, the flagship of the modern world. Through thick and thin, relentlessly, he strove to create the perfect museum, which would provide a complete encyclopaedia of the history of the arts, and in which all the branches of art of every era of human civilization could be studied from high quality examples. All this was not merely an end in itself, but in the thinking of the time was a prerequisite for the development of world-class contemporary Hungarian art.

In an exceptional felicitous moment in Hungarian history, Pulszky's passionate ambition met with political sympathy and generous financial resources. Hungary perhaps never experienced such an unfettered economic boom and optimistic mood as between 1867 and 1914; and very rarely have its politicians recognized the power of culture and the arts in national development as they did then. Thus in 1894 the Hungarian government agreed to Pulszky's plan for the creation of the Museum of Fine Arts, and set aside a vast sum, 3.6 million forints (more than the contemporary value of over two metric tons of gold) to realize it. This included 1.5 million forints earmarked for the construction costs of the new museum building, and 2.1 million forints for acquisitions for the collections.

The Italian Renaissance Room of the National Picture Gallery as installed in the building of the Hungarian Academy of Sciences, 1871.
(Watercolour by Gyula Háry)
Museum of Fine Arts, Budapest

Pulszky's opus was not conjured out of thin air – far from it. It rested on two pillars: one robust and strong, the other a little awkward, and yet indispensible. The first was the gallery of Hungary's most powerful, richest aristocratic dynasty, the princely Esterházy family, which the Hungarian state purchased in 1871. This collection was monarchic in nature, with a great many splendid masterpieces from the giants of the sixteenth and seventeenth centuries. But the gallery almost completely bypassed the "primitive" art of the centuries before 1500, the excessively frivolous French Rococo, and even the unsettling masters that strayed so far from the mainstream, like El Greco.

It is customary to characterize the Esterházy collection as being Goethean in taste, and indeed, it came into being when the entire continent hung on the words of that stern German dictator of taste: the turn of the eighteenth and nineteenth centuries. It was created by Prince Miklós Esterházy II (1765–1833), the most powerful noble in Hungary, a highly cultured and immensely rich aristocrat, for whom the gallery was not only a passion, a labour of love, but also an instrument of propaganda to raise awareness of the rank and prestige

Joseph Fischer, curator of the Esterházy gallery, in his atelier, 1808
(Engraving by Joseph Fischer)
Museum of Fine Arts, Budapest

Portrait of Archbishop János László Pyrker, 1842
(Painting by Miklós Barabás)
István Dobó Castle Museum, Eger

of his family. Accordingly, from 1814 the collection was open to the public in Vienna, the capital of the empire, rivalling with two other illustrious Vienna galleries: the collections of the imperial house and the Liechtenstein family. Almost from the moment it opened, the Hungarian public urged over and again that the gallery move to the Hungarian capital, yet the princely family long resisted. The transfer was finally effected in 1865, and six years later the gallery became the property of the Hungarian state. The purchased works consisted of 637 paintings, 3500 drawings and 51 000 prints: this profuse collection would hold its ground even today as an independent museum.

The Esterházy gallery was soon conflated with the other pillar of today's collection, the art collection of the Hungarian National Museum which, although it contained a few first-rate masterpieces, had a somewhat awkward character due to the circumstances of its creation. The only section of it to be in any way coherent was the contemporary Hungarian collection, which was enriched by regular purchases. European art in general was represented by the sumptuous collection donated to the museum by János László Pyrker, Archbishop of Eger (1772–1847) in 1836. This outstanding scholar, writer and prelate acquired most of the 194 paintings in 1820–27, when he held the seat of the patriarch of Venice. Accordingly, the majority of the works are from Venetian painting; this rich art is embraced at a splendid level of quality. The Pyrker donation thus became a milestone on the path to forming the Museum of Fine Arts: the museum gallery no longer played the role of being a collection of works of local interest, but staked a claim to being a repository of general culture. It is thus no exaggeration that Pyrker's contemporaries feted him as the creator of the "National Gallery".

A third significant group, which passed to the ownership of the new gallery after the Esterházy collection was purchased, was a further step on the path towards general universality. A donation of sixty-two paintings from Arnold Ipolyi, Bishop of Nagyvárad (1823–1886) of a series of outstanding works filled perhaps the most conspicuous gap in the collection: the then rediscovered "untainted, sincere" world of fourteenth- and fifteenth-century painting.

Károly Pulszky was made director of the gallery in 1884. The ambitious plan envisaging the Museum of Fine Arts included both the construction of a new suitably spacious building, and a far-reaching acquisitions policy. In the proposal priority was given to the development of the sculpture collection (mostly through plaster casts); from early painting the key fields mentioned for the redressing of shortcomings were fourteenth- and fifteenth-century Tuscan monumental painting, and the seventeenth-century Dutch masters. Seen with modern eyes, Pulszky's plan appears to be castles in the air, but in this era of optimism it actually became reality. The ceremonial founding of the Museum of Fine Arts took place in 1896, but Pulszky was able to start the large-scale purchases in 1893. Over the following two years he purchased 297 paintings, 142 sculptures, 50 drawings and 600 engravings, most of them excellent works.

King Franz Joseph at the opening of the Museum of Fine Arts, 1906
(Historical press photo)

His acquisitions went from medieval wellheads and Cretan icons to the paintings of Greuze, though they were preponderantly Italian Renaissance works. This album presenting major works features only occasionally one or two pieces purchased by Pulszky. Yet it is no exaggeration to say, as intimated above, that the Museum of Fine Arts is his opus. The unique character of the museum is after all given not by the highlights, the peaks that everybody knows well, but the contour of the plateaus surrounding the high points. Those excellent pieces which locate the peaks in interpretative, illuminating company, and thus reveal their true significance. Masterpieces almost never come into being as solitary cedars in the desert, but they grow even taller than the others in a rich, inspiring nutritional soil, in the midst of luxuriant vegetation. The unusual virtue of the Museum of Fine Arts lies in the fact that its rooms present a complete panorama of a given era.

Pulszky's fundamental principle of a general comprehensive collection remained the basic ideal of development in later decades too. Successors attempted to go further down this path, and make the museum even more universal. In 1906, on behalf of the Hungarian state, Bishop Péter Vay purchased in loco many hundreds of Japanese paintings, sculptures and woodcuts. Two years later, with the purchase of 135 marble objets d'art from German archaeologist Paul Arndt, a new chapter opened in the museum's collecting of ancient Greco-Roman art, which from this point on concentrated not on plaster casts of famous masterpieces of antique sculpture, but on the acquisition of original pieces. Meanwhile the collecting of Hungarian and world contemporary art continued in full swing, with large-scale lavish state purchases.

Hungary's exceptional economic and cultural development was arrested by the First World War, which had tragic repercussions for the country. With this the spectacular extension of the Museum of Fine Arts came to an end, and settled down into dedicated everyday work. Even after this the collection was of course enriched with important works from year to year, but no new trails were beaten out. The heroic era, formational for the basis of the collection's character, had come to an end. In the following decades two changes of

great importance took place, though both meant only the reorganizing of the existing state collections. The first was the Museums Act of 1934, pursuant to which the ancient Egyptian art treasures of the National Museum and the Ethnographic Museum would go to form the Egyptian collection of the Museum of Fine Arts; this would later develop into a comprehensive, world-class collection through the large excavations conducted by the museum's experts. At the same time the Ferenc Hopp Museum of East Asian Art, which until this time had been a branch of the Museum of Fine Arts, was given over to the Museum of Applied Arts.

The furthest-reaching event of the twentieth century, and also the most disorientating, is that as a solution to the permanent and increasingly acute lack of space the works of Hungarian art were removed in two phases and organized into an independent museum. First, nineteenth- and twentieth-century Hungarian artworks were moved to the newly founded Hungarian National Gallery in 1957, then in 1974 Hungarian art from the Middle Ages to 1800 was also transferred there. Today the situation is uncertain, but it seems that in some form the two collection will perhaps soon be unified once more.

Nowadays, the Budapest Museum of Fine Arts, like the other museums of the world, faces grave challenges. The world has changed radically. The traditional forms, paths and purposes of education and culture are undergoing a transformation. A museum can no longer be a temple dominated by reverence; it shall become a forum where every individual visitor seeks out his own personal interpretation of one work or another, and engages with it in dialogue, or even debate. In recent decades the relationship between visual culture and the book culture dominant for centuries, had been turned on its head: the museum, as the traditional guardian and expounder of visual culture, cannot allow itself to ignore this change of tide, nor indeed to fail to be and the vanguard of the shift. The museum has a key role in the public's mastering of the grammar of visual communication, of their learning to understand and use pictures to express their own ideas. The collections of the Museum of Fine Arts make it uniquely suitable for this task due to their wide range and variety.

Axel Vécsey

Cycladic civilization

Idol, c. 2700–2400 BC
Marble, height: 61 cm
Purchase from the Paul Arndt collection, 1908
4708

Lying to the east of the Greek mainland, in the isles of the Cyclades which are rich in marble (Naxos, Paros, Syros and Amorgos) the most striking works of early Bronze Age art are the marble idols. Most often they represent naked female figures with folded arms and their feet fixed down. The majority of the figurines were found in tombs, laid next to the deceased, but their precise function has not been identified. The Cycladic representation of the human body, radically different from classical art and with an emphasis on pure elements of form, also inspired several twentieth-century artists.

On the face of most idols the nose is the only detail defined, but the white surface was once brightly painted. On the Budapest piece to the right of the nose we can clearly see the formerly painted arc of the almond-shaped eye protruding from the surface. Above the right eye we can faintly see yet another eye, similar in size and shape: the idol was thus originally painted with four eyes. The ridge on the brow, also originally painted, may have been a hairband or a diadem.

The particular features of this statue are its large size and the richness of its painted decoration. Most Cycladic figurines are 20-40 cm high; an idol larger than 60 cm is rather rare. Of its painted attributes, the two pairs of eyes may have invested the statue with the ability to see all, and the diadem with power, so it perhaps depicts not a simple mortal, but some being with supernatural powers.

Szilvia Lakatos

Egypt, reign of Thutmosis III

Stele of Noferhaut, (1479–1425 BC)
Red standstone, 98 × 52 × 32 cm
Gift of Count János Waldstein, 1870
51.2143

This stele was purchased by Count Waldstein in Luxor. Its original owner Noferhaut, an officer of pharaoh Thutmosis III, set up the stele as a votive gift to the god Amun-Re. Noferhaut was chief of the medjai-troops (a type of desert police) and overseer of the foreign lands.

In the upper section of the stele an offering scene is depicted: Thutmosis III, Noferhaut's lord, is shown offering papyrus and lotus flowers to the god Amun-Re, king of the gods, whose figure appears seated on a throne in front of an altar.

In the lower section, the text of a hymn can be read. The hymn is addressed to Amun by Noferhaut, who is shown in front of the text with his arms lifted in adoration, and with various animals (fowl, gazelles and fish) hanging from a stick over his shoulders. The depicted animals are offerings to the god, and represent the entire cosmos (sky, earth and water) under the authority of Amun, and are also symbols of localities (marshland, desert, and water) which were regarded by the Egyptians as homes for the forces of chaos. By presenting these symbolic animals to Amun, Noferhaut affirms that he has fulfilled the task entrusted to him by the king, and seen to it that the desert and foreign regions are integrated into the ordered world ruled by Thutmosis III.

Katalin Kóthay

Egypt, New Kingdom
(1580–1085 BC)
Head of a Man, c. 1350–1290 BC
Limestone, height: 22 cm
Acquired from unknown source before 1934
51.2262

Towards the end of the Eighteenth Dynasty, in the Amarna period (c. 1353–1333 BC), profound changes occurred in Egyptian religious and artistic thinking. The new subjects and, somewhat naturalistic trend in art was a dramatic departure from the traditional, timeless Egyptian style. Very soon, however, in the subsequent post-Amarna period, artists returned to old subjects and methods. Yet some of the innovations persisted and influenced later art. This statue head, exhibiting traits of both traditional and Amarna art, was probably produced in the post-Amarna period. Consistent with the traditional style, the idealized face – though it represents a young man – does not actually reflect the age of its owner, nor his personality, or emotions. Yet the naturalistic rendering of the eyes and lips, as well as the form of the pierced earlobes, is reminiscent of Amarna art.

The superbly carved head may come from a seated or kneeling statue representing a man of high status. His titles and name were probably inscribed on the back pillar, the remaining small part of which preserves only a few signs of a two-column hieroglyphic inscription. Originally the head was painted, and it is documented that traces of red ochre were still visible on the face in the 1930s, when it was transferred to the Museum of Fine Arts from the Hungarian National Museum.

Katalin Kóthay

Egypt, Ramesside Period
(13th century BC)
Young Lady with the Standard of the Goddess Hathor
Crystal sandstone, 35 cm
Acquired from unknown source before 1934
51.2048

The statue fragment depicts a young woman. Her head is covered with a braided wig, the top of which is ornamented with a bunch of lotus flowers. She wears a decorative necklace and a gently pleated dress. She holds a divine attribute fastened upon a handle or a pole at her right shoulder, supported by her left hand. The attribute shows the human head of Hathor *en-face* with the ears of a cow. Her head is surmounted by a chapel façade, with the figure of a cobra rearing up (another representation of Hathor) in its entrance.

Hathor was one of the most important divinities of the Egyptian pantheon. Among her manifold appearances the most frequently represented is the cow, referring to her as universal divine mother who gives birth to the sun god and the pharaoh. When represented in human form, she is most frequently attributed with horns or ears of a cow, alluding to her divine maternal and regenerative power. The design of the divine emblem recalls those of votive sistra, ritual rattle instruments, which were one of the Hathoric symbols used by her priestesses during religious celebrations held in the temples of the goddess. In these rituals music and dance with erotic associations played an important role, and were believed to have regenerating power. During the New Kingdom female members of the royal family and court were closely linked with Hathoric rituals. It is thus highly probable that the owner of the statue was of noble origin and served as a priestess of Hathor during her life.

Éva Liptay

Egypt, 21st Dynasty
(c. 1069–945 BC)
Funerary papyrus
Papyrus, painted, 100 × 10 cm
Purchased in 1935
51.2547

The purpose of funerary papyri was to equip the deceased with all kinds of necessary information during his or her perilous journey to the netherworld which, it was hoped, would end in rebirth in divine form. Two deities played a particularly important role in these conceptions of the afterlife: the sun-god Re and Osiris, ruler of the netherworld. The papyrus contains no texts. Nevertheless, the strong semantic link among the four separate scene panels is as cohesive as the grammar of a verbal text. The artist was inspired by the *Netherworld Books* of the tombs in the Valley of the Kings at Thebes which depict the nocturnal journey of the sun-god.

In the first scene, the knives in the head of the serpent clearly show that the being depicted is Apophis, the defeated enemy of the sun-god Re. The serpents of the second and third scenes, however, are benevolent, and assist in the rebirth of the sun-god and the deceased. In the third scene the bird-shaped spiritual aspect (*ba*) of the deceased appears presenting an offering to the sun-god who is depicted in the solar barque (in the form of a *wedjat*-eye encircled by the sun-disc). The closing scene shows two scarabs and an ithyphallic divine figure. The locale is the mountain of the eastern horizon; at the moment before sunrise. The artist masterfully represents the last 'productive moment' full of tension, condensing all regenerative and creative energies into one point.

Éva Liptay

Egypt, 22nd Dynasty

(945–715 BC)
Anthropoid coffin of Dihoriaut, c. 750 BC
Wood, gesso, linen, 179 × 48 cm
From the Archiepiscopal Museum of Eger, 1950
51.1995/1–2

In the Egyptian concept of the afterlife, the soul left the body on death in the form of a bird (called *ba*), and joined the cyclical path of the sun god. In order to be reborn after death, it was essential for *ba* to periodically find its way back to the mummy lying in the burial chamber, and unite with it. Thus the coffin had to resemble as far as possible the deified state of the deceased, so as to be recognisable to the returning ba.

During the era of Libyan pharaohs (from the 10th century BC) the attitude toward death had become more passive. The fate of the deceased became more dependent on divine intervention than on the living, and, as a result, temples (and funerary statues within) gained a greater role in the funerary cult. Consequently, from the second half of the 8th century BC coffins were designed to emphasise their statue-like character with low pedestals under the feet, and back-pillars for the base. The central figure of the lid is the ram-headed, bird-bodied deity, the afterlife aspect of the sun god, protectively stretching out his wings over the deceased. The tail of the bird continues in a column of polychrome hieroglyphic inscription consisting of a short offering formula which divides the surface of the lid under the waist into two symmetrical halves. On each lateral zone run three scene panels with the figures of Osiris and protective funerary deities (the four Sons of Horus), and down below winged sun-discs provide magical protection and rebirth for the deceased.

Éva Liptay

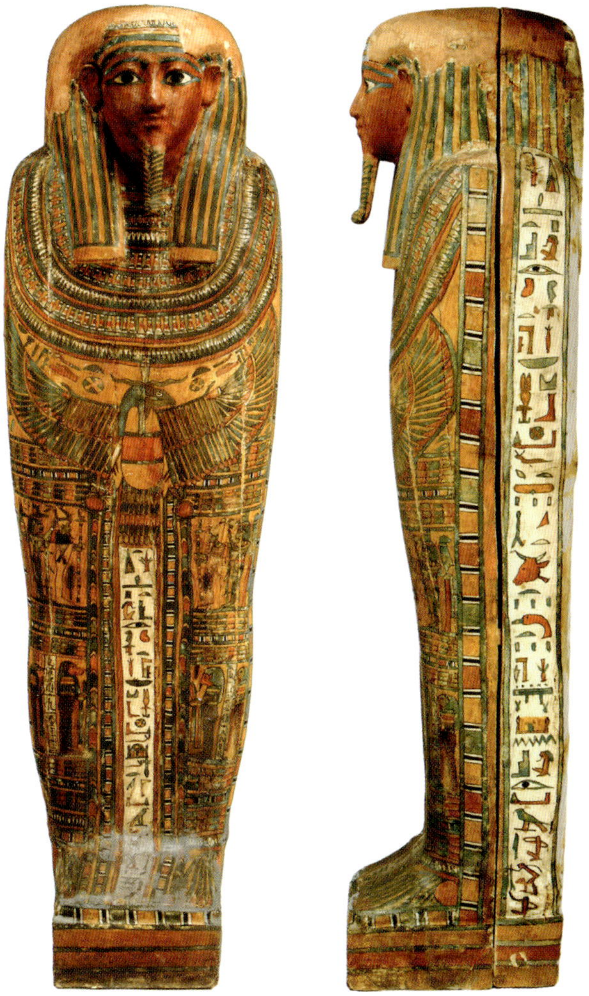

Egypt, 26th Dynasty
(764–525 BC)
Statue of Imhotep, 7th century BC
Bronze, with precious metal inlays, height 22 cm
Gift of Mrs György Ráth, 1906
51.2313

Imhotep lived during the Third Dynasty (c. 2686–2613 BC) of the Old Kingdom and was high priest of Heliopolis and architect of King Djoser's Step Pyramid complex, which was built at Saqqara. In later times he was regarded as a man of wisdom and the author of admonitions. From the Twenty-Sixth Dynasty, the so-called Saite Period (664–525 BC), onward he was revered as a god with his own cult and temple. His worship was most widespread in the country during the Ptolemaic period (305–30 BC), when he was equated with Asklepios, the Greek god of medicine. Many votive statues were dedicated to Imhotep to ask for his help and intercession in sickness and infertility, and in rebirth in the afterlife.

The Budapest Imhotep, a splendidly executed bronze with fine inlays of gold, electrum and silver, is an early and top-quality example of these votive statues, and according to the inscription written on its plinth, the statue was dedicated to Imhotep for the benefit of a man called Kham-Khonsu. Imhotep is represented seated on a chair with a papyrus scroll on his lap. The hieroglyphic inscription engraved on the papyrus asks for Imhotep's intercession with the god Ta-tenen, the personification of the afterlife.

The statue formed part of the Fejérváry-Pulszky collection as early as in 1842. By 1873 it came into the collection of György Ráth, whose widow presented the whole collection to the Hungarian state after Ráth's death.

Katalin Kóthay

Chiusi, Etruria

Cippus base, 5th century BC
Pietra fetida, height: 29.5 cm
Purchased, 2006
2006.2.A

In the 6th century BC Chiusi was one of the largest Etruscan artistic centers, and its stone carving workshops had their own special way of preparing tombs. The urns, sarcophagi, and the characteristic multipart funerary columns (called cippuses) were carved from the local limestone (which has a rather offensive smell, hence its name: "fetid stone") and were decorated with scenes related to burial ceremonies. This cippus base is carved on all four sides with excellently preserved reliefs showing scenes from funeral games. The sports are clearly recognisable: competitors in chariot and running races, wrestling, boxing, and athletes throwing the discus and javelin. Each competition is watched over by umpires holding the sign of their office, the fasces, consisting of a long rod and three branches; clerks write up the results. The games are accompanied by music, and to complete the show is a troupe of acrobats and masked Phersu figures (beings between the worlds of men and gods, who often appear in Etruscan feasts). Competitions held in honour of the dead were also customary in ancient Greece: in the 23rd canto of the Iliad, Achilles holds the games and offers the prizes himself in memory of his deceased friend Patroclus. The scenes depicted on this base appear in almost exactly the same form in artworks from other large Etruscan centres of the 6th and 5th centuries (tomb frescoes, vase decorations), so this may have been the customary programme for funeral games in Etruria.

Szilvia Lakatos

Egypt, 26th Dynasty

(764–525 BC)
Statuette of a cat, 7th–6th century BC
Bronze, height 15 cm
Gift of Mrs György Ráth, 1906
51.2356

According to the ancient Egyptians the gods could express either their destructive or their benevolent side to mortals. The ferality and playfulness typical of felines was expressed on the one hand by the unbridled ferocity and bloodthirstiness of the lioness (Sakhmet/Tefnut), and on the other by the benevolent effect of the cat goddess Bastet, placing emphasis on her domesticated and supple nature. Both aspects of the goddess are closely linked to the sun-god and solar concepts. According to the *Myth of the Solar Eye* she is the daughter of the god, (actually personifying the divine Solar Eye) who according to myth in a fit of anger transformed herself into the shape of a lioness (or a wild cat), and strayed into the remote South. The sun-god dispatched the baboon-shaped Thot in pursuit of her and he managed to bring her back in a domesticated and pacified cat form. The head of this statuette is carved with a scarab beetle (the rising form of the sun-god), referring to the animal's link with the sun-god. The eyes are inlaid in gold. One of the rock crystal pupils decorating the eyes has been lost.

During the first millennium BC the main religious centre of the goddess Bastet venerated in cat form was the town of Bubastis in the Eastern Delta. Herodotus gives a vivid account of the fertility ceremonies performed there. Hundreds of statuettes like this, obviously intended to represent the cult image of the temple, were presented as votive offerings to the goddess.

Éva Liptay

Andokides Painter

(active c. 530–515 BC)
Red-figure Kylix, c. 520 BC
Terracotta, diameter: 21.5 cm
From the collection of Antal Haan, 1950
51.28

In Athenian vase painting around 525 BC red-figure decoration appeared alongside the already customary black-figure style. The so-called Andokides Painter was among the pioneers of red-figure pottery, though he was trained in the black-figure tradition. The large amphoras for storing wine were his favourite vase type, and he decorated one side in the old technique, and the other with the new. He only made a few kylixes, which were used as drinking cups at banquets.

The anonymous artist was christened after Andokides, the potter who made and signed some of the vases decorated by him. He himself never signed his works, so they can be identified only by a thorough examination. The Budapest kylix is undoubtedly by the Andokides Painter: the characteristic profiles with a slightly protruding and sometimes downward-turning lower lip, the peculiar bulging shapes of the heads, the elbows and ankles are all features typical of him.

The Budapest kylix is markedly different from his other cups decorated in red-figure, as it is much smaller to those. Its size is usual for black-figure kylixes, as is the Gorgon's head on the inside of the cup. Decorating the outside with eyes also customary with black-figure kylixes, whereas on red-figure pieces alongside the eyes the palmette was an indispensible element. The Andokides Painter thus straddled two eras: he used the forms and part of the decorative system of black-figure pottery combined with the red-figure technique.

Szilvia Lakatos

Peloponnesian master
Grimani Jug, c. 450 BC
Bronze, height: 31.2 cm
From the Fejérváry–Pulszky collection, 1899
56.11.A

Gábor Fejérváry, with his nephew Ferenc Pulszky, created Hungary's most important private collection of ancient art. He bought this bronze jug, dating from the classical period of Greek art, from the collection of the Grimani family of Venice in 1833. Judging by the shape, the Grimani jug was used at banquets for decanting wine. The body of bronze vessels had formerly been cast, but by the fifth century BC they were hammered from sheet metal, and thus in spite of the use of common decorative motifs each piece was individual.

The tongue pattern running around the foot, the pearl-string-like ribbing following the arc of the handle and the palmette which closes it merely complement the two figures intended as the main adornments of this graceful jug. On the edge of the lip sits a bearded figure with pointed ears, holding drinking horns. This is Silenos, a companion to Dionysos, god of wine. Behind him, at the base of the handle, is a siren with wings spread. The ancient Greeks believed these woman-headed birds awaited those entering the Underworld, that with their enticing song they might soften the bitterness of death. The linking of wild revelry and death may seem odd, but it was not alien to Greek thought. They believed they would have parties in the beyond too, so the necessary vessels were often placed next to the dead. The Grimani jug, which is completely intact, was probably placed in the depths of a tomb shortly after it was made, to accompany its owner on his or her journey to the realm of Hades.

Szilvia Lakatos

Brooklyn-Budapest Painter

(active c. 380–60 BC)
Red-figure Nestoris, c. 370–60 BC
Terracotta, height: 42.4 cm (including handles)
Acquired by exchange, 1948
50.191

Red-figure vase painting developed in Athens about 525 BC. For the following century the masters of Athens pursued the technique with almost no competition. From about 430 BC however, vase painters and potters moved from Athens (entangled in a severe war with Sparta) to southern Italy, where Metapontion in Lucania became one of the Greek centres of vase-painting.

In spite of its Greek name, the nestoris is not Greek in origin. It was named in the nineteenth century after Nestor, whose goblet as it was described in Homer's *Iliad* resembled this form. However, it is actually a variation of a vase type of the Messapii, the inhabitants of the peninsula of Salento, in the south-eastern corner of Italy. The Greek potters were thus in contact with the local populace, and learnt from them, adapting to their needs. Though the form of the vase is of local origin, it is decorated with a typically Greek scene. In the middle sits the young god Dionysos, holding the thyrsus, a staff adorned with ivy leaves. On the left a female figure offers him a cup of wine. At the right edge of the scene a satyr leaning on a column serves to emphasis the Dionysian mood. Yet the ribbon encircling the two columns suggests that the scene is set before a tomb, in a burial-ground. In this case the image may depict the welcoming of the deceased into Dionysos's entourage, a religious belief popular in southern Italy. The vase may originally have been intended as a grave good, perhaps for the very female figure in the design.

Szilvia Lakatos

Egypt, Ptolemaic Period

(332–30 BC)
Relief fragments from a Ptolemaic temple,
c. 305–285 BC
Limestone, height 31 cm, width 96–142 cm.
From the excavation at Kom el-Akhmar, 1907
51.2156–60

The relief fragments once decorated the walls of a temple built at the beginning of the Ptolemaic Period at Kom el-Akhmar, near Sharuna in Middle Egypt. The Budapest fragments, together with other similar pieces now in Vienna and Cracow, were found in 1907 by an Austro-Hungarian expedition sponsored by Fülöp Back, a Hungarian merchant in Egypt. The reliefs depict and name the founder of the temple, Ptolemy Soter I, as well as gods and goddesses. The Ptolemies, who ruled over Egypt following the death of Alexander the Great, made it a conscious part of their religious policy to maintain the ancient religious institutions. By renewing and enlarging old temples or building new ones, they ensured the continuity of the cults of major Egyptian gods. The decorations of these temples show these rulers of foreign origin represented with traditional pharaonic attributes and insignia. Ptolemy I Soter and his son and successor, Ptolemy II Philadelphos (who probably also built at Kom el-Akhmar) provided funds for temple constructions at several major traditional cult centres all over Egypt. The building of the temple at Kom el-Akhmar, an important administrative and religious centre already from the 3rd millennium BC, can be seen as part of these religious policies. In earlier times the town was a centre of the cult of the god Nemty, venerated in the form of a dual falcon, while its Ptolemaic temple was dedicated to the local form of the cult of the falcon god Horus.

Katalin Kóthay

Greece, Hellenistic era
(c. 330 BC–1st century BC)
"The Budapest Dancer", c. 240–220 BC
Parian marble, height: 62 cm
Purchase from the Paul Arndt collection, 1908
4759

The statue known as the *Budapest Dancer* is one of the Museum of Fine Arts' most famous classical antiquities. It portrays a young girl as she pulls her cloak to one side and, leaning forward, looks before her feet. Its fame is due to its being one of the finest specimens of early Hellenistic (third century BC) sculpture. One of the main innovations of the period was the exploration of the artistic possibilities of the 'multi-view' compositions. In contrast to earlier sculptures designed for one single main viewpoint, the girl's movements can only be understood by revolving around the statue.

In the Hellenistic era it became common in public buildings and homes of the wealthy to erect statues with a merely ornamental function; the *Budapest Dancer* was probably made for such a purpose. Since the carving on the back of the statue is much rougher, it was clearly not intended for an all-round view, but before some background, for instance a niche. The subject of the statue is uncertain, as is the question of whether the girl is a mythological character or a mortal. She is traditionally considered to be a dancer, but her movements do not correspond to any of the known classical ways of imaging dance. On the basis of her forward-leaning motion she could be interpreted as a decorative figure for a fountain or pool, the portrait of a girl looking at herself reflected in the water. Equally, it may be one of the new genre scenes of the Hellenistic era, the girl gathering her clothes.

Szilvia Lakatos

Rome, Imperial Period

(27 BC–476 AD)
Detail of a Ceremonial Procession, c. 25–40 AD
Luna (Carrara) marble, height: 107 cm
Museum purchase, 2000
2000.14.A

At the end of a decades-long civil war, Octavianus, later to become Emperor Augustus, took power. He maintained the semblance of a republic, but with the help of a powerful propaganda machine, which made the mythical story of his family the origin myth of the entire Roman people, he created an autocracy. It is no coincidence then that the ceremonial chariots shown in the relief, used for transporting sacred objects of the state gods, are decorated with scenes that had been made the key points of Rome's ancient history. On one side of the chariot Aeneas, son of the goddess Venus, rescues his father and son from the fire devouring Troy, in order to set out on his journey that would lead to his new home, Italy. On the other side we see Romulus, the founder of Rome, with the weapons confiscated from the defeated enemy warlord. To position Aeneas, Augustus's mythical ancestor, alongside Romulus, venerated by Romans as the founder of Rome, and to make him his equal, was a contemporary political statement: it was intended to legitimize the rule of Augustus, who also proclaimed himself the scion of Venus.

The relief is part of a larger cycle which stood as a memorial of Augustus's victory at Actium in 31 BC, which put an end to the civil war. Part of the series depicted the battle at sea, and the other panels the subsequent celebrations. After Augustus's death he was venerated as a god, and temples were erected to him. The reliefs may have adorned just such a shrine serving for the cult of the emperor.

Szilvia Lakatos

Roman Empire, Province of Africa

Orpheus, 3rd–4th century AD
Mosaic, height: 97 cm
Museum purchase, 2004
2005.7.A

After the destruction of Carthage (146 BC) the central part of Northern Africa became the Roman province called Africa. Agricultural production in the large local estates played a crucial role in supplying the empire, so Africa became one of the richest regions. In terms of art too, the area was closely linked to the classical culture of the Greco-Roman world. For instance, the floors of wealthy villas were adorned with vast mosaics depicting stories from mythology. Orpheus was the most famous songster in Greek mythology. His singing and playing the lyre charmed even the gods of the underworld, who restored to him his dead wife, Eurydice. His music even subdued wild animals – this scene was a popular subject for Roman mosaics, with Orpheus in the centre, and round about the animals turning to face him. The Budapest mosaic may also have been the central part of such a large-scale composition.

Orpheus became especially popular from the beginning of the third century, in the late imperial period which faced the crisis of the empire and classical culture. By then the figure of the singer had been enriched with novel elements: for instance, he was thought to be the originator of a Greek religious belief which aimed to secure the soul's prosperity in the afterlife. The image of the divine singer thus offered countless possibilities of interpretation, which varied according to era, region and intellectual persuasion. In fact, his figure was adopted unchanged by Early Christian art as one possible form of representation of Christ.

Szilvia Lakatos

Maso di Banco

(c. 1300–1350?)
The Coronation of the Virgin, c. 1333–38
Tempera and gold on wood, 51.2 × 51.7 cm
Gift of Lord Rothermere (London), 1940
7793

In *The Divine Comedy* Dante predicted that Giotto's then brilliant reputation would be but a fleeting glory. He was wrong: in vain did new more eloquent or passionate masters come; to this day Giotto is venerated as the father of modern Western painting. It is no wonder then that the British press magnate Lord Rothermere, who was put forward as a possible heir to the Hungarian royal throne, felt that a fitting donation to 'his people' would be a fine, characteristic Giotto, which depicted a coronation scene to boot: the inauguration of the Virgin Mary as Queen of Heaven. And though the crown did not finally go to the Englishman, and the picture is no longer considered to be by Giotto but by his most excellent pupil Maso di Banco, its outstanding value has indubitably remained.

Here we see the essence of Giotto's stylistic revolution. It is said that he translated the language of painting from Greek (i.e. Byzantine) to Latin, and his rational style is indeed rooted in the spirit of classical antiquity. The ultimate theme is the harmonical order which reigns in the created world: this is suggested by both the calm mood free of pathos or emotional fervour, and the clear, rational geometrical structure. This latter is unified by the new method of representing space, linear perspective, the system which would define for centuries the way Western art saw the world. Unlike with the icons, in this system the scene is seen from a single, personal viewpoint, making the beholder the very centre of the picture's microcosm.

Axel Vécsey

Czech (?) artist

Saint Margaret, c. 1410–15
Brush, black ink, black and red chalk, grey wash,
21.4 × 14 cm
Esterházy collection, purchased in 1871
1

In the chaotic time of the political and ideological decline of the late Middle Ages a wealth of art sprang forth. The art of around 1400, international Gothic, conquered all the important ruling centres of Europe simultaneously: courts of kings, dukes and nobles. Prague, the new imperial residence of the Holy Roman Emperor, was then at its zenith. Late Czech Gothic infiltrated not only nearby towns, but made its influence felt in the whole of Central European art.

The Budapest *Saint Margaret,* drawn with soft lines in the elegant pose of the "Beautiful Madonnas" so popular in international Gothic art, is probably the work of a Czech master. Madonnas and saints curved in a gentle S-shape, radiating tenderness and calm, often appear on panel pictures, as book illustrations and as statues. This Saint Margaret, her mantle falling in deep folds and shaded with a high degree of plasticity, may have been intended as a model for a sculpture. Medieval masters did not generally work directly from nature, but gleaned inspiration from earlier works of art. The pattern sheets which preserved popular motifs were greatly respected in the workshops, and jealously guarded. However, very few drawings from this period are known. The Budapest *Saint Margaret,* which is in surprisingly good condition, and is unusually large for the era, is a rare, fine work of High Gothic art.

Zoltán Kárpáti

German or Prague sculptor

Beautiful Madonna, c. 1430
Painted limestone, 124.5 × 43 × 32 cm
Purchased in Frankfurt, 1916
4967

European art around 1400 took on a uniform stylizing decorative style which swept away the differences between the various artistic centres. This style, which appeared simultaneously in many important centres in Europe and affected all branches of art, is now known as International Gothic. The lyrical, soft elegant style of late Gothic is perhaps most strikingly embodied in the contemporary Madonna statues, which were known as Beautiful Madonnas on account of their main characteristic, the idealized charm suggestive of supernatural beauty. This outstanding statue is one of the best known of the Beautiful Madonnas. Typically for this type, here too the Virgin is shown with a conspicuously young face, a tall crown, and her markedly emphasized S-bend body is covered by a softly draped ample cloak carved into tubular pleats.
Identifying the place where the Beautiful Madonnas were made, in the uniform style that infused all of European art, is usually a very tall order. In the case of the Budapest sculpture, bought on the Frankfurt art market, even the provenance is doubtful. Thus it has been associated with almost every important artistic centre of the time: it has been considered a Rheinish, Silesian, or Salzburg work, but most likely seems an origin in the Prague region. Equally debatable is the time it was sculpted. While it was initially compared to early Madonnas produced around 1390, it is now held to be rather a work from the close of the period, at about 1430.

Miriam Szőcs

Sassetta

(c. 1400–1450)
Saint Thomas Aquinas in Prayer, c. 1423–25
Tempera and gold on wood, 23.6 × 39 cm
Gift of Arnold Ipolyi, 1880
32

"You have written well of me, Thomas" said the vision of Christ, according to the legend, to Saint Thomas of Aquinas, when he prayed for a sign of whether what he had written was true. The last great painter of the lyrical Sienese Gothic school, Sassetta's brush brings to life with a kind of "magic realism" the enchanting world where the believer engages in intimate discourse with the divine sphere day by day. The saint now pleads for inspiration in front of a household altar, and his prayer is answered: Christ embodies in golden light and sends to him the dove of the Holy Spirit. The miracle takes place in the interior of a monastery, brought to life with many familiar details. The codices left open on the desks remind us the friars who used to fill the library with life. In the background a view opens onto a garden and within it a fountain, the centre of everyday life in the monastery. This tiny masterpiece comes from a polyptych's predella, the horizontal base supporting the larger pictures. The altarpiece was commissioned by the Sienese guild of wool merchants, and was kept locked in a cupboard in the guild's headquarters. Each year however on the feast of Corpus Christi it was erected in front of the building, and an open-air mass was celebrated before it to the participants in the procession. The tradition lasted until the sixteenth century, when the altarpiece was moved into a church. Finally it met the fate of so many medieval polyptychs: it was sawn into pieces and sold to art collectors.

Axel Vécsey

Michele Pannonio

(c. 1400–1464)
The Muse Thalia, c. 1456–57
Tempera and oil on wood, 136.5 × 82 cm
Gift of Arnold Ipolyi, 1880
44

The wealthy urban bourgeoisie of Renaissance Italy liked to take refuge from the summer heat or epidemics in their countryside villas. As Boccaccio recounts in the *Decameron*, here they would relax, with instructive and amusing stories, music, dance and witty conversation – in other words, they paid tribute to the muses. It was no coincidence, then, that they often adorned the walls with pictures of the muses. This was the case in what was perhaps one of the most famous summer retreats, the dukes of Ferrara's villa Belfiore ('beautiful flower'), where this picture comes from.

Michele Pannonio's name suggests that he was from Hungary (Pannonia). He may have been a friend of another famous Hungarian in the court at Ferrara, the poet Janus Pannonius, whose master Guarino da Verona devised the concept for the muses' at Belfiore. The surviving text reveals that here we see Thalia, who is shown in the role of the muse of agriculture rather than the patroness of comedy. This is indicated by the motto at the bottom of the picture (*'I taught man to plant'*), and also the mature ears of wheat surrounding Thalia's head, the bunch of grapes in her hand, and the luxuriant fruit surrounding her throne. Her pregnant state, unusual for the muses, further reinforces the idea of fertility.

The willowy form of Thalia's body, her graceful curves and soft contours recall late Gothic taste. The lilies and swags of fruit, painted with robust naturalism, are more modern in style: they may have been painted by the gifted rival of Pannonio's, Cosmè Tura.

Axel Vécsey

ΦΥΤΕΙΑΣ ΓΕΝΟΜΟΥΣ ΑΠΕΜΟΥ ΔΗΓΝΩΤΕ ΓΕΩΡΓΟΙ
PLANTANDI LEGES PER ME NOVERE COLONI

Gerard David

(c. 1460–1523)
The Nativity of Christ, c. 1485
Oil on panel, 76.6 × 56.5 cm
Purchased in Cologne, 1894
1336

Gerard David was the last great master to practise the stylistic tradition of Early Netherlandish painting that originated with Jan van Eyck. This is a curious art, with a radically different approach to that of Italian contemporaries, who incidentally were enthusiastic admirers of Northern paintings; indeed, it was from these that they picked up the knack of painting with oils. But this technical innovation, which charmed onto the surface a vitreous shine like a transparent precious stone, is only one of countless means with which these pictures enchant the receptive viewer. The aesthetics of 'small is beautiful', the meticulous and affectionate execution of every minute detail of the depicted world, is what makes this refined style so vivid.
The jewelbox-like town of Bruges, where David settled as a young man, looks as if it were the essence of this tradition. Here worked the most eminent painter of the time, Hans Memling, whose elegant, courtly style exercised a decisive influence on the youth. As the cityscape visible in the background is enlivened with all manner of small details, so the story is enriched with all kinds of episodes, in order to bring the miracle closer to the viewer, that it be more directly experienced. For instance, the candle in Joseph's hand reminds us that actually it is night, though the light radiating from the newborn shines bright as day over the landscape. The young shepherd in a yellow cape bears the painter's own features.

Axel Vécsey

Hans Holbein the Elder
(c. 1465–1524)
Death of the Virgin, 1491
Oil on oak, 150 × 228.5 cm
Gift of Ferenc Kleinberger, 1911
4086

The Bible tells us little about the life of the Virgin Mary. People of the Middle Ages, however, wanted to know more about the woman who had become a focus of religion, and the supreme heavenly intercessor for the created world. Thus many apocryphal legends were born, and these episodes eventually appeared in church pictures. One of the most important stories was Mary's death. It is said that Jesus protected the body of his mother from earthly decay, and took her body and soul into heaven, where she was crowned Queen of Heaven. Medieval preachers often compared Mary's body, the vessel for the Redeemer, to the Ark of the Covenant, which 'was of acacia, for that is incorruptible and the worms do not chew it away. Thus the body of the Virgin is worthy of being saved from corruption.' Although today he is chiefly remembered as the father of the brilliant Hans the Younger, in his lifetime Holbein the Elder was also greatly esteemed. The *Death of the Virgin*, replete with small details taken from everyday life, is one of his most splendid works. The Virgin, with her unperishing young body prepares mildly for the end. The actions of the apostles gathered around the bed are consistent with the actual rite for the dead: Saint Peter sprinkles her with holy water, Andrew swings incense, and John puts a candle in her hand, the symbol of a peaceful death. Three read the scriptures, one of whom is, anachronistically, wearing spectacles. Meanwhile above the gate of heaven opens, and Jesus beckons his mother come hither.

Axel Vécsey

Tilman Riemenschneider
(c. 1460–1531) and workshop
Virgin and Child, c. 1505–10
Painted limewood, 116 × 37 × 25 cm
Purchased in Frankfurt, 1923
5898

Tilman Riemenschneider ran the largest sculpture workshop of his time, where with the help of over forty apprentices he fulfilled countless commissions. Not only were his works admired, but in time he was also elected a member of the town council of Würzburg. His unparalleled rise to fame ended in 1524–25 with the German Peasants' War. Würzburg council sided with the peasants, so when the uprising was put down Riemenschneider too was incarcerated, and although he was soon set free in the years that followed he no longer received important commissions. Riemenschneider belonged to the last generation of German Late Gothic, and he raised woodcarving to a masterly level, introducing quite a few innovations too. Monochrome unpainted wooden carved altars were disseminated largely through his works. In addition, his workshop was a model of organization. Because he worked simultaneously on several commissions, the workshop produced one kind of sculpture for up to decades, almost unchanged in form. This Madonna is one of the popular types carved often, of which eight other versions are extant. They follow the pattern so closely that in addition to drawn designs it is conceivable that carved models were also used. Other evidence for this is that several small Riemenschneider wooden sculptures of barely half a metre high are extant, which may have had just such a role in the shop.

Miriam Szőcs

Wolf Huber

(c. 1485–1553)

Landscape with Willows and Mill, 1514

Pen and brown ink on paper, 15.3 × 20.7 cm

Esterházy collection, purchased in 1871

191

In the early sixteenth century a small group of Austrian and German artists developed a special interest in nature. The 'Danube school' was not a movement in the traditional sense: the term covers artists who depicted the Danube river valley and Alpine landscapes in the same spirit and style. Although they were all painters, it was primarily in their drawings that they created a new genre in German Renaissance art. Their drawings, which show mainly dense woodland and high mountains, are the earliest examples of independent representation of nature. The most famous exponents of the 'Danube school' are Albrecht Altdorfer from Regensburg, and Wolf Huber, a native of Austria who worked in the court of the bishop of Passau.

The date on the Budapest sheet reveals that Huber made this lyrical, virtuoso pen-and-ink drawing around 1514, while travelling in the Alpine region. Showing trimmed willows lining the winding road and the watermill next to the brook, it may once have belonged to Huber's sketchbook. The bare branches sketched with calligraphic lines, and the treetrunks shaded with small, dense penstrokes, lend a particularly decorative quality to the composition. Huber's contemporaries were fond of copying his 'land portraits', and the works influenced engravers too, including Augustin Hirschvogel. A contemporary drawn copy reveals that the Budapest composition was originally wider: a considerable part of the right side is now missing.

Eszter Seres

Luca della Robbia

(1399/1400–1482)
Christ and Saint Thomas, c. 1463–65
Terracotta with traces of the original painting,
44.5 × 22 × 12 cm
Purchased in Berlin, 1916
4974

The craftsmen, artists and doctors of Florence attempted to defend their interests by forming guilds. They located the guilds' headquarters in the robust Gothic edifice originally intended as a market and wheat warehouse, the Orsanmichele, the facade of which was adorned with statues of each of the guilds' patron saints.

In 1463 the merchants' tribunal (Tribunale della Mercanzia) took over the statue niche of the Guelphs, a political party that supported the guilds, and commissioned Luca della Robbia, one of the most sought-after sculptors of the early Renaissance, to design a large statue group depicting Christ and Doubting Saint Thomas. As was custom at the time, the master made a small terracotta (fired clay) model of the planned monumental bronze. The apostle Thomas, doubting the resurrection, placed his hand in Christ's side (John 20:24–29), thus gaining proof that Christ had indeed died, but was risen again. (The judges may have interpreted this story as a metaphor of their vocation: to 'play the doubting Thomas' until tangible evidence is found.) The scene is not dynamic; rather it is as if time stood still for the moment when Thomas accepts what for the human mind is incomprehensible.

The model, however, failed to please the commissioners, because in the end the bronze was cast not of this composition, but of one by another leading sculptor in the city, Andrea del Verrocchio. That group, far more dramatic, dynamic and monumental than Luca's, can be seen to this day in Florence.

Manga Pattantyús

Domenico Ghirlandaio

(1449–1494)
Saint Stephen the Martyr, c. 1492–94
Tempera on wood, 191 × 56 cm
Purchased in Paris, 1914
4914

Domenico Ghirlandaio's shop, which employed many assistants (including the young Michelangelo), was the largest art company in Florence at the end of the fifteenth century, and practised not only painting, but jewellery, mosaics, and who knows what else. With Ghirlandaio's activity being so multifaceted, he was open to absorbing all the influences around him. No other of his Florentine contemporaries was as touched by Netherlandish painting, and nobody adopted its achievements with greater understanding than he. The painstaking details of the drawing, with a pin-sharp brushtip, the deep glow of the colours, betray the Northern influence in this image too. The first Martyr of Christianity, stoned to death a few years after Jesus's crucifixion, Saint Stephen appears with such transfixing power in three-dimensional realism, which for the contemporary viewer must have been shocking. Perhaps it was to dampen the effect, or in turn to reinforce it, that Ghirlandaio placed the figure in a feigned niche, and with this transposition, a painting imitating a statue imitating a live human being, he blurs the line between fiction and reality even further. The panel was originally part of the high altarpiece of the church of Santa Maria Novella, which was painted on both sides and could be viewed from all round. There it stood in the centre of the choir, surrounded by one of the greatest achievements of the Florentine Renaissance, Ghirlandaio's celebrated fresco cycle of the lives of Mary and Saint John the Baptist.

Axel Vécsey

Leonardo da Vinci

(1452–1519)

Studies of Heads for the Battle of Anghiari, 1504–1505
Black and red pastel on paper, 19.1 × 18.8 cm
Esterházy collection, purchased in 1871
1775

Study of a Head for the Battle of Anghiari, 1504–1505
Black and red pastel on paper, 22.6 × 18.6 cm
Esterházy collection, purchased in 1871
1774

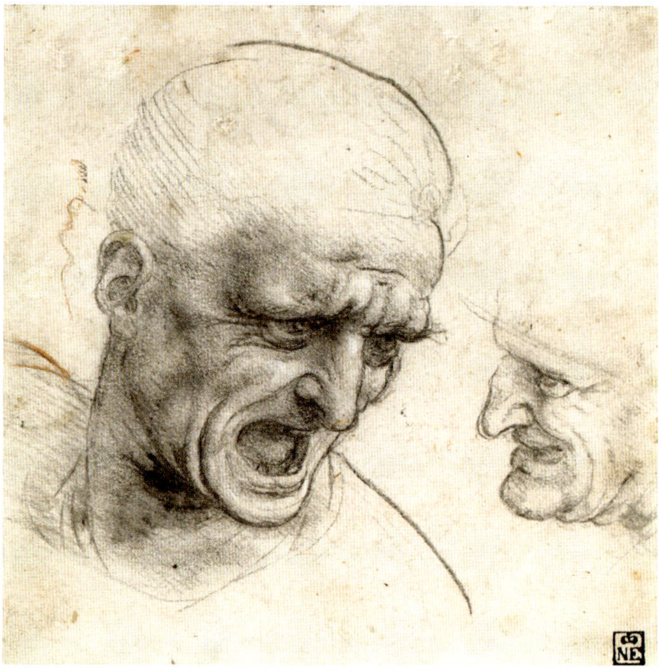

Leonardo was already over fifty when he was commissioned to decorate one of the long walls in the great hall in the Palazzo Vecchio, the Florentine town hall. The specified subject was the victory gained at Anghiari over the old rival Milan in 1440. Although such a prestigious commission must have been flattering to the painter, and his younger rival Michelangelo was working on a pair to the fresco, Leonardo once more began to work only after prolonged hesitation. Rather than the traditional fresco technique he experimented with a special slow-drying method, but met with failure. He had not yet finished the central scene when, in the poorly heated dank room the fresco began to decay. After this Leonardo abandoned the work completely, and a year later left Florence for good. While the fresco, which fell victim to subsequent alterations to the hall, is known through several contemporary reports and copies, barely half a dozen drawings for the work in Leonardo's own hand survives. Made in the last stage of the preparations, these head studies, with their vividness for being done from a live model, their dramatic expression, the highlights and deep tones creating the characteristic Leonardine chiaroscuro contrasts, count as some of the master's most excellent drawings. They also faithfully convey the staggering horror of the soldiers' cruel warring fury as they rush at each other with unbridled ferocity in the heat of battle, a state Leonardo called *pazzia bestialissima*, the most bestial madness.

Zoltán Kárpáti

Leonardo da Vinci ?

(1452–1519)
Equestrian Statuette, first half of the 16th century
Bronze with green patina, 28 × 24 × 15 cm
From the bequest of István Ferenczy, 1914
5362

Leonardo was trained in the workshop of Florentine sculptor Andrea Verrocchio, then won many prestigious commissions for sculptures. However, apart from contemporary accounts, a few autograph notes and many magnificent drawings very few traces remain of Leonardo the sculptor. His two monumental equestrian memorials ended in failure. The huge clay model for Francesco Sforza's equestrian statue in Milan, finished in 1493, was destroyed by the French invaders, and the Trivulzio funeral monument got only to the planning stage.

It would be tempting to compare the Budapest statuette with these failed Leonardine equestrian monuments, but its origins should be sought elsewhere. The type of the Budapest equestrian can be found in the preparatory drawings for a fresco in the Florentine town hall, *The Battle of Anghiari*, begun in 1503 but later destroyed. In one of these sheets an annotation by Leonardo indicates that he used small wax figures to compose the complex, dynamic battle scenes of the fresco. The model for the Budapest statuette must have originally been just such a small-scale wax figure, which in the process of enlargement lost something of the dramatic tension apparent in the drawings. The invention, the extravagant twist of the horse as it rears up, and the vigorous dynamic composition of the rider, certainly derive from Leonardo. It is not however known whether the master himself had a hand in casting the small bronze, or whether it was done by an apprentice.

Miriam Szőcs

Giovanni Antonio Boltraffio
(c. 1467–1516)
Virgin and Child, c. 1495–97
Oil on poplar, 82.4 × 63.4 cm
Esterházy collection, purchased in 1871
52

Leonardo da Vinci warned his fellow artists: 'No one should ever imitate the style of another because he will be a grandson rather than a son of nature.' But it seems that in his own workshop he did little to encourage his pupils to develop their own style. All over the world there are many Madonnas and portraits which only under the scrutiny of a practised, expert eye reveal that the brush that painted them was held not in Leonardo's own hand. This is particularly true for this *Madonna* which is said to be 'the finest Leonardesque picture not painted by Leonardo himself' – although some scholars believe the master may, after all, have guided the hand of his best pupil, Boltraffio, during the execution. The picture is perfectly Leonardesque in every respect: there is the famous sfumato, or the delicate shading softening the outlines of the forms, the Virgin's enigmatic smile and her characteristically large hands, and the pyramidical composition. Indeed, it was recently revealed that the wood on which it was painted was hewn from the same log as Leonardo's London *Madonna of the Rocks*. Yet the most Leonardesque part is the basic idea: the Christ Child reaches for something which has already disappeared, and it is forever a mystery to the viewer what the object might have been. It was once thought that the picture was unfinished, and that the master planned to paint a rose in the fine faience bowl, but technical examination has proved beyond doubt that this is the finished state.

Axel Vécsey

Raphael
(1483–1520)
Esterházy Madonna, c. 1508
Tempera and oil on wood, 28.5 × 21.5 cm
Esterházy collection, purchased in 1871
71

Right up to the end of the 19th century Raphael was honoured as the unsurpassable peak of painting: the master who recreated the spirit of classical antiquity and transcended its achievements. The timeless harmony, serene palette and peerless grace of his pictures served as a model for centuries. And if since then the public has come to feel closer to tortured geniuses wrestling with themselves, if the struggling torso pleases more than final perfection, the fact remains: every idea and aspiration of the Italian Renaissance reached its culmination and attained perfect synthesis in the art of Raphael. In spite of being left unfinished (the Virgin's face and the figures of the children remain in the underpainting phase), the *Esterházy Madonna* represents the most perfect moment even of this absolute art: the end of the Florentine years, before Raphael moved to Rome where he would move on and begin to deconstruct the harmony. It is still the season of synthesis, and as if the express intention was to pay hommage to his predecessors, the posture of the Madonna was developed from Leonardo's paraphrase on an admired classical statue (the *Crouching Venus*). The pyramidal geometric structure, which masterfully directs the viewer's attention to the scroll held by Saint John the Baptist, also derives from Leonardo's ideas. If the picture reached completion, this scroll would bear John's prophecy on Jesus's role as redeemer: 'Behold, the Lamb of God, who takes away the sin of the world!'

Axel Vécsey

Gentile Bellini

(1429–1507)

Caterina Cornaro, Queen of Cyprus, ca. 1500

Oil on wood, 63.2 × 49.3 cm

Gift of János László Pyrker, 1836

101

The heroine of Donizetti's opera, Caterina Cornaro was not born to the crown. The Venetian patrician girl was swept to the throne of Cyprus by her legendary young beauty and the caprices of politics. Rather than ruling, her role was to become a moral example – so decided Venice, which wanted the important trading post for itself. Thus she abdicated from the throne, but in exchange became the most feted celebrity in the city, a strange and exciting curiosity: a queen in the republic. When the leading Venetian master of the time, Gentile Bellini created this celebrated portrait, the bloom of her youthful beauty had waned. The painter makes no bones about this, and approaches his model with cartographical objectivity. The sumptuous gala dress is given as much attention as the face. The intricate rhythms of necklaces, veils, fabrics and jewels seem to combine to form a kind of eastern ornamental pattern: like those that Bellini studied so enthusiastically during his years at the Istanbul court. The braiding seems to symbolize the restraint of duty: it seems to fetter the woman, biting into her flaccid flesh, while she stands firm, without so much as a tremor. This makes the image an epitome of the ruler's virtues: the dual triumph over external challenges and selfish inner desires. And this makes it the very masterpiece claimed by the confident words put into the mouth of the queen in the inscription: *'You see how great I am; but even greater is the hand of Gentile Bellini which portrays me on such a small panel.'*

Axel Vécsey

Giorgione
(c. 1478–1510)
Portrait of a Youth ('Broccardo Portrait'), c. 1508–10
Oil on canvas, 72.5 × 54 cm
Gift of János László Pyrker, 1836
94

'Even today it is difficult to define what the advent of Giorgione means for the history of taste. Like Proust, he taught that the world could be looked at in a more pleasurable, more subjective way. His recipe for doing so was to infuse painting with the lyricism and romance that were already current in the prose and poetry of his time.' It would be hard to find a better summary of Giorgione's significance than the words of the great art historian John Pope-Hennessy. Though he died young, Giorgione utterly overturned the world of Venetian painting, and enshrouded not only narrative scenes in a magical, poetical atmosphere, but also transferred this approach to portraiture. So was born the introspective, emotive type of male portrait, of which the most inspired example is the Budapest *Youth*. Yet the image is also the most perplexing image in our collections. Its author and sitter are the subject of endless dispute, as are the meaning of the hieroglyphic emblems on the parapet, and even the very nature of the emotion which infuses the picture. Is the sitter in a reverie, tormented by the bittersweet pain of love, or does he exude some quiet melancholy from the depths – perhaps grief? Perhaps the painter captured a hallowed moment of religious devotion or poetic inspiration? Some even claimed it may be an inauguration into some secret society. Of course there is no objective answer: everyone interprets the mood according to his own inclinations. One thing is certain: nobody can resist the picture's spell.

Axel Vécsey

Albrecht Dürer

(1471–1528)
Portrait of a Youth, c. 1500–10
Oil on pinewood, 43 × 29 cm
From the Habsburg imperial collections, 1848
142

Rider with a Lance, 1502
Pen-and-ink drawing on paper, 27.2 × 21.5 cm
Esterházy collection, purchased in 1871
75

Albrecht Dürer was indisputably the greatest sixteenth-century painter north of the Alps. Not only did he have a God-given talent, he was also an exceptionally deliberate and self-aware master. He travelled round Italy several times, thoroughly working through everything important, and making use of what he considered good. But he found his home tradition more beneficial, and since the theoretical basis was lacking, he decided to create it. 'The more rigorously your work adheres to life, the better it will appear. So you should never wonder whether you could do better than that with which God has endowed the natural world he created,' runs Dürer's alternative to the idealising Italian aesthetics.

In the small painted portrait he did not wish to 'correct' the work of nature, the strange, asymmetrical smile of this young German. How right he was! For it is precisely this lopsided smile that is the key to the aura, which makes the man enigmatically interesting, but also magically alive. A host of scholars have claimed for decades that the mysterious smile could only have been inspired by Leonardo, yet it is an integral outcome of Dürer's own principles.

The *Rider with a Lance* does however reveal that behind the apparently artless naturalism there was actually thorough research of the proportions of the human body. This splendid study drawing, bursting with life, was very likely made from live models, but two tiny holes betray that a pair of compasses was used in drawing the outline of the horse.

Axel Vécsey

Barend van Orley
(c. 1488–1541)
Portrait of Emperor Charles V**,** c. 1519
Oil on oak, 71.5 × 51.5 cm
Purchased in Cologne, 1894
1335

Emperor Charles V, perhaps the most powerful ruler of all time, had an empire on which, it was said, the sun never set. He ruled over Spain, Germany, the Low Countries, Southern Italy, and had extensive colonies in America and Asia. His portrait was painted by the greatest artists of Europe, from Dürer to Titian, so that through copies of the portraits, albeit metaphorically, he could be present in every corner of his empire. Yet Charles was not a particularly attractive man, as attested to by contemporary accounts: 'His lower jaw is unwieldy and protrudes, as if it were not a natural part of him, but some additional imitation; and so if he closes his mouth, a space the size of a row of teeth is left between the upper and lower teeth.'
One of Charles's first portraitists was Barend van Orley in Brussels. This image was made about the time the adolescent young man had been elected (at the cost of enormous bribes) Holy Roman Emperor. However, there is no reference here to this title or to the Spanish throne he had inherited earlier; only the royal emblem of Burgundy, the flint and steel, appears on the large hat brooch, between the large doubled initial of his name, and around his neck hangs the badge of the famous order of the golden fleece. Van Orley created an ideal fusion of Northern and Mediterranean styles to lend an imposing realistic air to his portraits: the forms of the body are captured with masterly Italianate plasticity, while the jewels and clothes have a Netherlandish richness of detail.

Axel Vécsey

Andrea Riccio ?

(1470–1532)
The Rape of Europa, c. 1520
Bronze with green patina, 18.2 × 16.5 × 7.5 cm
From the bequest of István Ferenczy, 1914
5363

Zeus, the untiring seducer, took on the image of a tame bull in order to draw near to the Phoenician princess playing on the shore with her companions. After the bull, bedecked with flowers, had managed to trick the beautiful Europa onto his back, he swam across the sea to the island of Crete. In the oft-depicted Ovidian version of the story however there is no mention of the pugnacious resistance apparent in the Budapest small bronze. In Ovid's *Metamorphoses* the princess was quite taken by the overtures made to her by Zeus turned bull. It is likely, then, that the author of the Budapest sculpture took inspiration not from this popular work, but from a less well known ode by Horace, in which the Roman poet writes of Europa's desperate protestations.

This is the only cast known of this small bronze, and although the identity of its author remains doubtful, the unusual choice of source betrays he was familiar with Humanist works. The style of this outstanding piece is closest to the works of Andrea Briosco, given the sobriquet Riccio (curl) after his dense, curly hair. Riccio, known for his excellent bronzes, nursed close relations with the Humanist circles of the prestigious University of Padua, and influenced by this made a whole series of classically inspired small bronzes. Renaissance small bronzes are now considered sculptures, but at the time many were intended as functional objects. Such is the *Europa*, the interior of which is designed to hold incense.

Miriam Szőcs

Sebastiano del Piombo

(1485–1547)
Portrait of a Man, c. 1512–14
Oil on panel, 115 × 94 cm
Purchased in Milan, 1895
1384

Thanks to Giorgione's new style Venetian painting rose to become the greatest rival in Italy to Tuscany. News of it spread to Rome too, and thus one of his best pupils, Sebastiano, received an invitation to the papal court. Here he came under the spell of Michelangelo's classical, epic heroism, which he tried to combine with the leisurely poetry inherited from Giorgione. And when Michelangelo left for Florence, and Raphael died a couple of years later, Sebastiano became Rome's leading painter.

This extraordinary portrait, perhaps of a scholar, was painted shortly after he arrived in Rome. The Venetian legacy still predominates: in spite of the man's tangible, monumental presence he seems to fade in from the mist of some nostalgic poem. The soft atmospheric effects and the twilight hues cast an enigmatic aura about him, although in the rigorous composition Sebastiano had already departed from his master.

Piombo's masterpiece is one of the greatest achievements of Renaissance portraiture. But Károly Pulszky, founding director of the museum, was vilified for the purchase, and finally driven to suicide. Pulszky acquired the picture as a Raphael, and his witless political opponents thought that the quality of a work of art is determined by the reputation of its author. The *Portrait of a Man* is today one of the emblems of the museum, and perhaps this fact may serve as a late appeasement for the excellent connoisseur, and as a memento to the public that lives under the spell of 'great names'.

Axel Vécsey

Jacopo Sansovino

(1486–1570)
Virgin and Child, c. 1510–11
Wax, gilt canvas, 65.5 × 23.5 × 19 cm
Purchased in Florence in 1895
1177

When the sculptures adorning public spaces in Renaissance Florence were commissioned, the artist was often selected by an open competition. The participants had to make a model sculpture from clay or wax, which was judged by a jury consisting of artists, town aldermen, or delegates from aristocratic families. This small-scale sculpture by Jacopo Sansovino was made for just such a competition.

Around 1510–11 it was planned to erect a marble statue of the Madonna on the facade of the market Mercato Nuovo, and Sansovino entered the competition with this wax model. Because wax is highly malleable, it was particularly suitable for making models: if the artist wished to alter the form, he simply had to warm it, and he could add or remove the material as he pleased. One unusual technical feature of the statue is that the bodies of the two figures are not supported by an armature. They were so cleverly composed by Sansovino, who was both a sculptor and an architect, that they support one another with their own weight. The artist dipped the drapery serving as the Virgin's attire in glue and coated it with a layer of wax of varying thickness, then covered the surface of the entire statue in gold.

Although this maquette won Sansovino the competition, the commission went not to him, but to a rival with political connections, Baccio Bandinelli. Sansovino's winning entry must then have passed to one of his painter friends, Andrea del Sarto, who used it as a model for two works.

Manga Pattantyús

Correggio
(c. 1489–1534)
Virgin Suckling her Child, c. 1522–24
Oil on panel, 68.5 × 56.8 cm
Esterházy collection, purchased in 1871
55

'No craftsman ever painted with greater delicacy, such was the softness of his flesh painting, and such the grace with which he finished his works' wrote Giorgio Vasari, in his chronicle *Lives of the Artists*, of Correggio. Later writers were just as enthusiastic. Stendhal was moved to tears by one of his works, and even flint-hearted Goethe was touched by the beautiful Correggio he saw in 1787 at an art dealer's in Naples. He wrote: 'it shows the mother of God with the Child at the very moment when the babe hesitates between the mother's milk and some pears proffered by a cherub. The theme is thus the weaning of Christ. The idea is most tender, and the delightfully executed composition is dynamic, natural, and splendid.'

The picture, which had passed through famous collections and was widely admired, could not of course be bought by Goethe, only by an immensely rich and refined collector like Prince Miklós Esterházy. For the lines above refer to the Budapest *Madonna* – indeed, it could not be put better today. Scholars have recently argued that the picture attempts, through an intricate system of symbols, to express the dogma of the Immaculate Conception. It may does, but even at that time only the most erudite and initiated believers would have understood. The simple viewer both then and now truly sees in the image but this deeply humane, vivid moment of motherhood, the weaning of the child. A theme that befits nobody so perfectly as Correggio's intimate, emotional style.

Axel Vécsey

Parmigianino
(1503–1540)
Venus Disarming Cupid, ca. 1527–30
Pen, ink and wash on paper, 18.8 × 14.3 cm
Esterházy collection, purchased in 1871
1890

Although during his brief two-decade career Parmigianino painted very little, few of his contemporaries had so marked an influence as he did. His popularity was largely due to the fact that his tastefully elegant style reflected with self-evident unaffectedness the ideal of beauty shared by the young generation of Mannerists who followed Raphael. Parmigianino liked to draw, and produced many drawings: more than one thousand of his sketches survive, and one of the finest of these is *Venus Disarming Cupid*. In the *Metamorphoses* Ovid tells of how Cupid once wounded his own mother, Venus, with an arrow, and she fell in love with the athletic but mortal hunter, Adonis. Thus the goddess of love came to know all the anguish of consuming passion. On this finely detailed Budapest sheet Venus is shown plucking away the unguarded bow from the child. The goddess is a masterful example of the *figura serpentinata* beloved of Mannerist and Baroque artists, a figure in unnatural, calculated elegant serpentine twists.
We do not know Parmigianino's purpose in making the drawing, but the coloured ground of the paper, the richly toned wash and the marked whitewash are akin to the preparatory drawings for his woodcuts. Though no contemporary woodcut version is known of, the Budapest drawing may be one of those Parmigianino made for the woodcutter Antonio da Trento in Bologna.

Zoltán Kárpáti

Agnolo Bronzino

(1503–1572)
Venus, Cupid and Jealousy, c. 1550
Oil on panel, 192 × 142 cm
Gift of István Keglevich, 1863
163

'The human eye cannot see like this,' stated Wölfflin, the authoritative art historian, of Bronzino's art. And perhaps a healthy human mind cannot think so crookedly as Bronzino's did, for this bizarre picture is able to jolt even today's jaded viewer. A blatant dissonance lies between the brazenly indiscreet erotic content and the annoyingly restrained form. There is body, but no soul, no instinct, no passion, no torrid arousal. There is no flesh, for bodies are hard as marble and cold as ice, as every outline is mercilessly sharp – this is what Wölfflin meant. Nor is there blood in them, they are blindingly white, like gesso (indeed, that is what they are made of: the gesso ground vibrates from beneath the thin, transparent colours). The tyranny of intended artifice weighs the picture down with sadistic overtones. The subject is no less contrived, in that the precise meaning of the picture, and that of its famous twin, the *Allegory* in the National Gallery in London, will perhaps never be unravelled. Whereas in the London image jealousy and fraud seem to triumph over love, here, in turn, desire seems happy, mutual, and the hideous monstrosity of Jealousy scurries away in the background. But in the laboured world of Mannerism, nothing is so simple. When looked under infrared light, it turns out that in the place of the children Eros and Anteros, representing requited love, there was originally a satyr baring its teeth with a demonic grin, similar to the mask beneath their feet.

Axel Vécsey

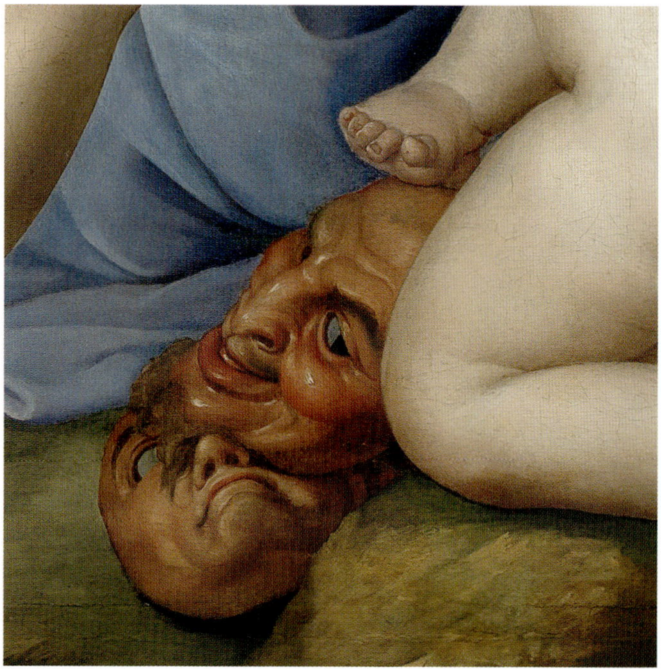

Hans Baldung 'Grien'
(1484/85–1545)
Adam and Eve, 1524–25
Oil on wood, each 208 × 83.5 cm
Purchased in Vienna, 1900
1888, 1889

Sixteenth-century Europe loved scintillatingly provocative pictures of women twisting men round their little fingers with cunning stratagem, thereby driving them to destruction. Particularly fond of the theme of the demonic power stemming from female sexuality was Hans Baldung, perhaps Dürer's best pupil, who was dubbed 'Grien' after his favourite shade of metallic green which here covers the snake's body. The obvious prototype for the role is Eve, the ancestral mother. Through her eating of the fruit, sinful but sweet to taste, the human body became the source of knowledge and pleasure, but also subjected to death. Baldung's pair of pictures (originally part of a series complemented by Judith with the severed head of Holofernes, and Venus and Cupid) focuses clearly on the story's erotic content. The sin is already done, the progenitors cover their loins with leaves, but their movements are wanton rather than shy. Evil has triumphed. Adam is tormented by lust: his body convulses, and he presses his right hand to the place of his missing rib. The locks of his hair form horns, his lips are parted, and his face is covered by a beard and moustache – all traits of contemporary depictions of satyrs. While Adam is portrayed as a victim, Eve is the active seductress, who finds unabashed pleasure in the power of her desirable beauty. The smile playing on her lips reflects self-satisfaction; her gaze and her every movement are directed to the man's body, as if to take possession of it.

Axel Vécsey

Lucas Cranach the Elder

(1472–1553)
Salome with the Head of Saint John the Baptist, 1530s
Oil on panel (poplar), 87 × 58 cm
Esterházy collection, purchased in 1871
132

The painter prince of the Protestant Reformation, Lucas Cranach was a close friend of Martin Luther, and also the godfather to his children. He made the illustrations of Luther's Bible translations, just as he did his portraits and allegories of his theses. Still, he had no qualms about providing his Catholic clients with pictures suiting their own faith, nor did he baulk at ribald subjects. Of course, we can if we wish interpret his piquant works as moral parables, which point out man's destiny if he surrenders to his lecherous desires. Indisputably, though, the host of Salomes, Judiths and other demonic women of fate that swarmed from Cranach's studio owed their popularity rather to their thrilling sensuality. They are icy, sadistic and triumphant, in the extreme attire of classy ladies of the time, and what is more they are endowed with the facial features of the illustrious beauties of the Wittenberg court.

Salome's name is not mentioned in the Bible; her bizarre cult was born only in the sixteenth century, to be revived by the decadent aesthetics of the late nineteenth century. Strictly speaking she was little more than a tool for her mother Herodias to get revenge on Saint John the Baptist, who had spoken out against her sinful relationship with the king. The payback came during a banquet, when Salome performed a maddening dance, and prompted by her mother, asked the spellbound king for her reward: John's death. She then handed her mother the disembodied head on a platter.

Axel Vécsey

Paolo Veronese
(1528–1588)
Portrait of a Man, c. 1555
Oil on canvas, 120 × 102 cm
Bequest of János Pálffy, 1912
4228

"There is one man who makes easy what we have always been told is impossible; and that is Paolo Veronese. In my view he is the only man who has penetrated the whole secret of nature," praised Delacroix his great predecessor. And indeed, in superior virtuosity, in graceful elegance perhaps only Tiepolo could compete with Veronese in the history of painting. He wallowed in formal tricks, yet remained classical in his spirit: his colours are pure as crystal, and create clear harmony; the locations are spacious and bathed in light; and underlying all the flamboyant cavalcade is a perfectly balanced geometric structure. And if others received more praise in the form of verse or statues, perhaps there was no painter whose direct influence was greater in the following centuries. This portrait of a young man posing in a sumptuous lynx fur not only conveys the dense essence of Veronese's genius, but also that of the aristocratic cultural milieu which was the hotbed for his art. The structure appears infinitely simple, and the execution also seems effortless, yet so many little ruses create the unquestionable air of authority about the man. His direct open gaze, his easy posture (as recommended by contemporary manuals of ambitious courtiers) is the embodiment of nonchalance. The character is shown through gesture, and just as the painter proclaims his model, he announces himself too: this confident, vigorous, yet easy manner of painting suggests a person born to absolute dominion over matter.

Axel Vécsey

El Greco

(1541–1614)
Penitent Magdalene, ca. 1576–78
Oil on canvas, 156.6 × 121 cm
Gift of Marcell Nemes, 1921
5640

It was said of El Greco that he painted with a piece broken off a wooden cross, without making any corrections, so that 'every patch of paint corresponds to God's will'. The story is not factual, yet it speaks volumes: it is as if the febrile visions evolved from the roughly defined, impetuous forms at the touch of some mystic power. Yet it is not, after all, God's hand at work, but their painter's passionate faith and talent, which forged a new organic unity from Christendom's two great painting traditions. Domenikos Theotokopoulos from Crete was already a recognized master of the old-style icon painting before he was captivated by the modern western style of Titian and Tintoretto. Wherever fate took him, to Venice, Rome and finally to Spain, in his soul he remained 'El Greco', 'the Greek'.

A former harlot, Magdalene turned to Jesus's most devoted believer. Following Titian, Greco condensed her story into the single moment of ecstasy: the moment when she, meditating in the wilderness on death and immortality, converts. But while for Titian her passionate revelation is accompanied by erotic overtones, here the blinding beam of light seems to purify her, almost uplifting her from the bonds of corporeality. The skull, which refers to earthly mortality, has rolled out of her hand, and behind her ivy, symbol of eternal life, stretches heavenwards. The dawn landscape, bathed in cold moonlit pale tones, is a delicate echo of the emanating experience of spiritual catharsis.

Axel Vécsey

Pieter Bruegel the Elder
(c. 1525–30 – 1569)
The Sermon of Saint John the Baptist, 1566
Oil on wood, 95 × 160.5 cm
From the Batthyány collection, 1951
51.2829

'The peasant': this is the name that has become associated with Pieter Bruegel the Elder, the greatest genius of sixteenth-century Netherlandish art. Not that he tilled the land (he was an erudite townsman), nor simply because he took pleasure in portraying peasant life with sympathetic irony. Yet his pictures do indeed seem to smack of the earth, for he had a worm's-eye view of the world. He was interested not in the heroes from the grand stories of mankind, but in what simple folk grasp of events, and how they affect them in everyday life. For sure, sometimes the conclusion is that they remain unaffected, as in the famous Brussels picture, *The Fall of Icarus*, where the ridiculous rebellion of man remains an imperceptible speck in the divine order. Not so in the *Sermon of Saint John the Baptist*, a key work in his oeuvre. Here the whole world draws up, in captivating diversity: nobles, priests, soldiers, burghers, peasants, Flemings, Spaniards, Jews, Gypsies, Turks, the healthy and the infirm. Yet this story tells not of differences, but of togetherness, of the new covenant that Christ would make with all mankind, and of the words of the prophet, by which it is foretold. This experience in common surges throughout the colourful throng, and resonates in their souls. Every sense is pervaded by the recognition that this is a special moment; that the Redeemer, as the prophet says, stands there in the crowd, and if he has not yet announced himself, the time when he will do so is near.

Axel Vécsey

Hendrick Avercamp
(1585–1634)
Frozen River with Skaters, c. 1610–15
Oil on oak, diameter 30.5 cm
Purchased in Paris, 1899
1698a

A decisive moment in the history of European painting was when during the sixteenth century artists first dared to paint pictures with no 'history'. No saints, no Greek gods: just a forest clearing, a shepherd driving his flock, or a table laid with food. Such a picture was a self-contained world, free of all literary references. And as new genres were born, so they soon had their specialists. Avercamp was the first Dutch master to specialize in winter landscapes, populated with many small figures, merrily sliding and skating. The popularity of this deaf and dumb painter peaked in the 1610s, in the decade where several exceptionally harsh winters visited the small town of Kampen, where he spent most of his life.

The inquisitive eye can delight in many charming little episodes within the refined structure of the Budapest picture too. A peasant pushes his wife and child on a sledge; figures in noble attire play *ijskolf*, the ancestor of ice-hockey; further back two gentlemen make towards a horse-driven sleigh. Many folk are skating, but not everyone is practised in the sport: one lad has fallen flat on his tummy on the ice, and lost his hat. Those who like ribald jokes can chuckle over the woman squatted down by the prow of the ship to relieve herself, while a dog bustles about her bare behind. The noble, the fisherman and the peasant take pleasure together, and perhaps this is the picture's underlying message: the unity of the newly independent Dutch nation.

Axel Vécsey

Leonhard Kern

(1588–1662)
The Three Graces, 1625–50
Stained limewood, 63 × 46 × 22 cm
Purchased in Budapest, 1926
6145

Like many of his fellow northern artists, Leonhard Kern travelled to Italy as a young man, where he spent no less than five years. The stations of his study tour were more unusual: as well as Rome he visited Naples, northern Africa and Ljubljana. Later he settled in Schwäbisch Hall in southern Germany, where he ran a large workshop. His career was overshadowed by the Thirty-Year War (1618–48), which almost completely prevented him receiving major commissions. Thus Kern was one of the first to start working for collectors and art dealers. His small-scale ivory, alabaster and wooden statues enjoyed particular popularity among his contemporaries.

More than half a metre tall and carved from several pieces of limewood, the Budapest *Three Graces* occupies a special place in the sculptor's oeuvre. Portrayals of the Three Graces of mythology grew popular in Renaissance Italy through the influence of classical art. The most favoured model was the Hellenistic marble *Three Graces* group, known through a Roman copy, which was installed in the Piccolomini Library in Siena in 1503. This may have inspired Kern's wooden sculpture, which somewhat differently to the prototype shows the female figure on the right not with her back, but frontally. Kern was fond of making nudes, which were inspired by both his experience in Italy and the female figures of Rubens. The three nudes in the Budapest group are linked by their arms with brilliant technical skill.

Miriam Szőcs

Peter Paul Rubens

(1577–1640)
Albert Rubens, the artist's son, c. 1619
Black and red chalk, pen, ink and wash on paper,
24.6 × 20.2 cm
Esterházy collection, purchased in 1871
1745

After several years in Italy Rubens returned to Antwerp, and was soon became the most authoritative painter not just of his homeland, but of the whole of northern Europe. His reputation was further enhanced by his unique diplomatic career. While he commuted almost ceaselessly between the courts of Europe's monarchs, his many painting commissions were completed by a sizeable team in his well-organized workshop. Most often Rubens's work was restricted to the preparatory sketches and the final brushstrokes. Like many of his contemporaries Rubens too was fond of depicting members of his family. Here he represented with special tenderness Albert, his son of about four from his first wife, Isabella Brant. The drawing was made in two clearly distinguishable phases. Rubens first sketched the main features in black and red chalk. Later he delicately reinforced the contours and more important details of the face in pen, and finally coloured the hair with brown ink, indeed so firmly that the original chalk lines can hardly be seen. In all likelihood this reworking is by Rubens himself, the reason for which may have been practical: he often used likenesses of his family for figures in his paintings. The Budapest portrait of Albert can be recognized almost unchanged as Saint John the Baptist in the *Madonna with Penitent Sinners and Saints* (Gemäldegalerie Alte Meister, Kassel), and as the putto in the lower right-hand corner of the *Madonna Surrounded by a Floral Wreath* (Alte Pinakothek, Munich).

Eszter Seres

Anthony van Dyck

(1599–1641)
Portrait of a Married Couple, c. 1617–18
Oil on canvas, 112 × 131 cm
Esterházy collection, purchased in 1871
754

The 'Mozart of painters', Van Dyck was barely more than a child when his fame spread. Like a firework he shot up into the heights, and turned out a host of brilliant masterpieces with ease, until finally he burnt out before his time, and the dazzling grand finale apparently never came. While still a teenager he produced celebrated works, and he was merely eighteen when he painted this *Married Couple*, a sure-handed masterpiece betraying superior technical skill and mature insight into human nature. Another Mozartian trait in Van Dyck is that he shone even when his hands were tied by the wishes of clients. He resented almost all his commissions being for portraits, but it was in this genre, which leaves least space for creativity and is thus held in disdain by critics, that he created his greatest works. The focus of Van Dyck's portraits is not the face, which is always bathed in a haze of melancholy; that is a mask belonging to the role assigned on the stage of society, worn with obedience, rather than the true mirror of the soul. Far livelier and more revealing are the hands: they divulge the character, and tell tales about the heroes. The traditional symbol of marriage, two interlinked right hands are here joined so as to display proudly the woman's valuable diamond engagement ring. Pride, tenderness, trust and care are condensed in this single gesture. And although the sitters have passed the bloom of youth, it is possible the picture commemorates a recently married couple.

Axel Vécsey

Niccolò Renieri

(c. 1588–1667)
Card-players, c. 1620
Oil on canvas, 174 × 228 cm
Esterházy collection, purchased in 1871
610

At the beginning of the seventeenth century, it was in Rome that the artistic heart of all Europe beat. Everyone who was anyone thronged there from every corner of the continent to see the masterpieces of antiquity, and the modern classics Raphael and Michelangelo, who eventually surpassed the ancients. But on arriving there, quite a few pupils were more enchanted by radical contemporary movements, particularly the provocative art of Caravaggio, and quickly forgot the classical greats. Perhaps it is no coincidence that the legacy of Caravaggio was first taken on by the young artists from the North (Holland, Flanders, France), whose home traditions laid closer to his naturalistic approach than those of the Italians, who pursued the celestial copy of reality. One of them was the French Nicolas Régnier, who grew up in Flanders. The monumental *Card Players* is the epitome of all that the northern youths did to transform what they inherited from Caravaggio. We rove through a decadent world, where ancient greatness has ebbed, and antique marbles are used as drinking benches. There are no upright heroes, only wily tricksters and foolish simpletons roam the ruins. All manner of parasites from nocturnal life – card tricksters, palm-readers, pickpockets, courtesans – have gathered here to rob the victims posing in fashionable clothes, their gaze all the emptier for that. The merrymakers mourn not the loss of the fortune squandered this night, but their entire, wasted, lives.

Axel Vécsey

Diego Velázquez

(1599–1660)
Tavern Scene, c. 1618
Oil on canvas, 96 × 112 cm
Purchased in London, 1908
3820

There are many who are considered *one* of the greatest, but far fewer who are thought to be *the* greatest. In the history of western painting, besides Raphael, Titian and Rembrandt only Velázquez belongs in this club. Manet called him the "painters' painter", and Picasso painted a host of paraphrases to uncover his secret. The essence of his magic was perhaps put most aptly by a contemporary writer, Francisco de Quevedo: Velázquez did not mimic reality, he created it. In this *Tavern Scene* and similar youthful *bodegons* (kitchen or tavern scenes named after the *bodega*, or inn) naturally the Spanish genius does not unfold in full maturity. Common folk populate the canvasses, in apparently banal situations, as if pages from the picaresque novels of Quevedo and his peers had come to life, where the larks of crafty servants and other villainous ruffians tickled the readers' fancy. This startling naturalism often invited claims of Caravaggio's influence, but at the time Velázquez had not even seen the pictures of the Italian vagabond. Even more importantly, in Velazquez there is no trace of Caravaggio's violent coarseness, however vulgar the subject may be, and a kind of calm, puritanical solemnity vibrates in the air. We can only guess at the exact story behind the image, but whether we see them as scheming gaol-birds or characters from an 'exemplary story', the figures' presence has weight and significance – no less so than the kings who populated the works of his mature period.

Axel Vécsey

Pieter Claesz.
(1597/98–1661)
Still-life, 1647
Oil on oak, 63.6 × 88.3 cm
Purchased in Vienna, 1889
1026

As if the table had been cut out of the previous Velázquez picture, the Dutch Pieter Claesz.'s still-life adopts the same tricks of the trade: the knife protruding over the edge of the table (to create the illusion of space), the crisply ironed white tablecloth with a sharp crease, and the virtuoso contrast in the quality of matter – shiny against matt, greasy against dry, hard against soft. The similarity is by no means coincidental, since formally both pictures derive from the same tradition: that of portrayals of the Last Supper, Jesus's farewell to his disciples and the institution of the Eucharist. The still-life is thus awash with religious connotations, and these associations are reinforced by various traditional Christian symbols (bread and wine, the vineshoot entwined around the wineglass, and the cruciform window frame reflected in the surface of the glass).

Though born in Antwerp, Pieter Claesz. was one of the 'most Dutch' painters. No other images better epitomized the puritan, Protestant national character than his simple 'Lenten still-lifes'. This ensemble of bread, wine, fruit and pie is not among his most ascetic compositions. The extravagance of the forsaken fruit pie signals the futility of earthly plenty, thus introducing a secondary layer of symbolic reference. Yet the overall mood is quiet and restrained, and this is mostly due to one indispensible component of Claesz.'s painting: he dulls the colours until he attains an almost monochrome palette.

Axel Vécsey

Jusepe de Ribera

(1591–1652)
The Martyrdom of Saint Andrew, 1628
Oil on canvas, 206.1 × 177.7 cm
Esterházy collection, purchased in 1871
523

Seventeenth-century Naples was, according to many, hell upon earth. Impoverished by Spanish rule, the life of the people was embittered by continuous starvation, epidemics, earthquakes, and even the Vesuvius. The hovels of the poor were increasingly crowded, since the scant harvests had forced village folk into the city. Crime flourished in the stale air of the back streets. It was perhaps inevitable that Caravaggio's violent art, which grappled with the fear of death, came into its own in Naples, and for decades it set the way for the city's painters. But the school of ruthless naturalism did not reach its peak until a generation later, with Ribera. This Spanish-born master was most in his element when portraying the tortuous deaths of Christian martyrs, with shocking verisimilitude, as in this masterpiece of his darkest period. The apostle Andrew preached the gospel in the East, until Roman governor of Achaea condemned him to follow the founder of his "superstitious sect" in death by crucifixion. If anybody, it is Ribera who manages to convince us that for Andrew martyrdom was redemption. His humiliated body is shrivelled by time, his withered skin hangs drily from his frame; and yet there emanates from him a metaphysical power of the soul. Over him tower shadows of a priest and the governor, presaging Goya's oppressive demons. They are not satisfied with destroying his body: to the very last moment they try to win over his soul, and persuade him to worship the idol of Jupiter.

Axel Vécsey

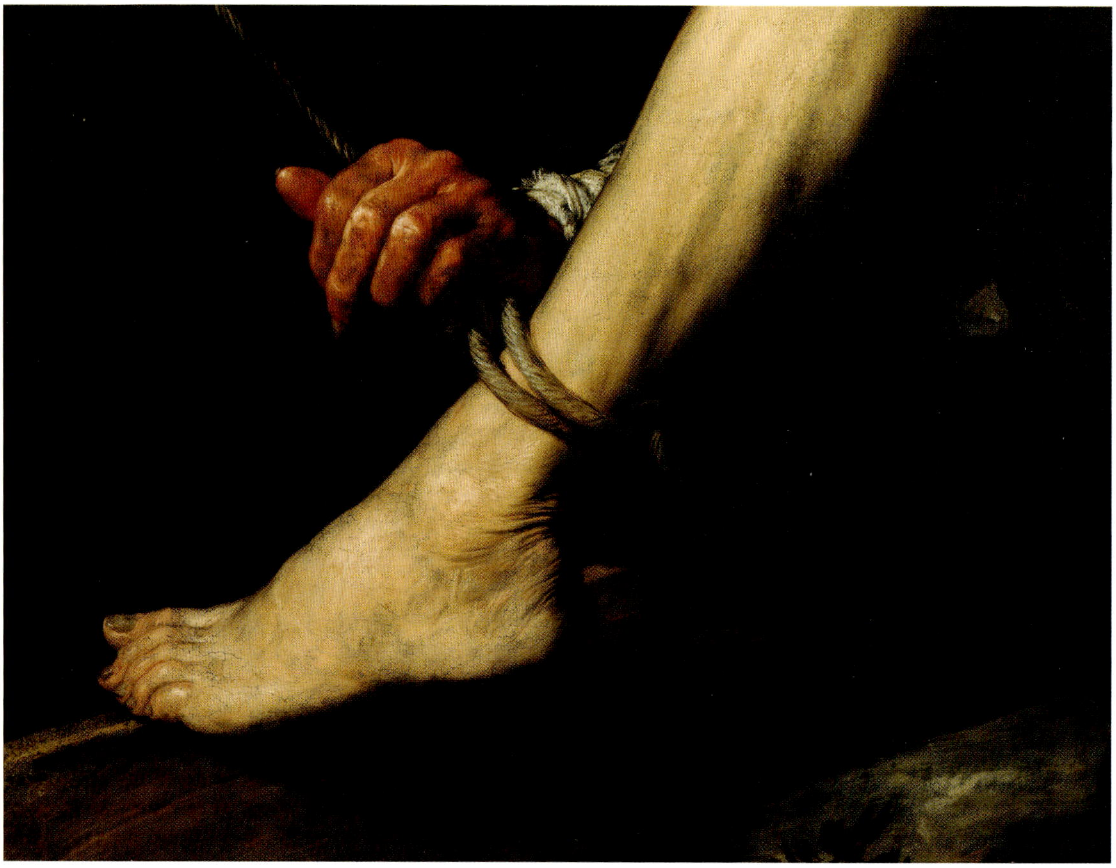

Daniele Crespi
(1597/1600–1630)
Saint Cecilia, 1620s
Pen and brown ink over black chalk on paper,
27.6 × 37.8 cm
Esterházy collection, purchased in 1871
2396

Daniele Crespi lived a mere thirty years, falling victim in 1630 to the plague raging in his native Milan. In spite of his brief career he left behind one of the most exciting oeuvres of the Lombard Baroque. This was the period when art in Italy changed radically under the pressure of the Counter-Reformation movement. Crespi trained in the workshop of the Mannerist Giulio Cesare Procaccini, famed for the idealized beauty of his works, but the pupil's brush soon turned out religious paintings conceived in the spirit of the Synod of Trent, full of dramatic realism and passionate emotions.

The Budapest Saint Cecilia is one of the most picturesque of his extant drawings. This saint died a martyr's death for her Christian faith in the third century. Since the Middle Ages she has been venerated as the patron saint of musicians, and she enjoyed especial popularity in the century of the Baroque. From the almost impenetrably dense vigorous, agitated penstrokes emerges a sketch whose expressive power is due mainly to the dynamic manner of drawing. Crespi achieved this through the highly inventive use of chalk and pen: flying in the face of contemporary technique he made not only the preparatory drawing in chalk, but also used it to reinforce the darker tones over the finished pen-and-ink drawing. The purpose of the work is not known. Not only the subject however, but the symmetrical scheme of the sheet suggests that perhaps it was made as a design for painted organ shutters.

Eszter Seres

Nicolas Poussin

(1594–1665)
The Holy Family at Rest, ca. 1627
Oil on canvas, 57 × 74 cm
Purchased in Budapest, 1957
57.18

Poussin is a painter at whom everyone marvels, but perhaps nobody likes. Nor was it his wish to be loved by the public: he declared that painting should address the mind, not the eye or the heart. Alongside Descartes he is the best known exponent of rationalism, the stony seventeenth-century French movement that stubbornly believed that perfection is attainable if we bend the world to the rules of reason. Poussin held the task of art to be that of staging the noble deeds of man in a logical system, as would happen in an ideal world.

However, this dogmatic rigour is barely discernible in the Budapest *Holy Family*. Of all Poussin's pictures it is perhaps the freshest, where we can even detect traces of tender emotions. But in this case the exception indeed proves the rule: this liberated mood is carefully calculated. Poussin consciously applied the theory of modes from the ancient aesthetics of music, in which the theme determines the particular emotional tone and the order of dramaturgy. But a refined, elevated melancholy is mixed into this serene idyll, as the child Saint John the Baptist proffers a palm cross to Jesus. This toy, prefiguring the child's horrific earthly fate, links the picture to one of the main themes of classical drama, the conflict between feelings and duty. The disciplined resignation of child and mother sets a model for the noble, wise handling of such conflicts.

Axel Vécsey

Bartolomé Esteban Murillo

(1617–1682)

The Infant Jesus Distributing Bread to Pilgrims, 1678

Oil on canvas, 219 × 182 cm

Esterházy collection, purchased in 1871

777

To this day there still hangs a copy of the Budapest *Jesus Distributing Bread* in its original location, a former rest-home for elderly priests in Seville. Murillo's masterpiece enjoys their admiration not merely for its captivating, gentle charm, but also because it would hardly be possible to express more perfectly the mission of the institution. The vision of Jesus distributing bread reminds us of the Christian's duty to care for those who fall by the wayside, a duty that originates with Christ himself. Yet it affirms this with a self-evident naturalness free of any didactic overtones. The viewers thus experience the duty of mercy not as a chore, but as an inner spiritual compulsion which they willingly obey. It was precisely this intimate immediacy and warm empathy which was the secret of Murillo's popularity, which in the eighteenth and nineteenth centuries rivalled Raphael's. Perhaps today the Spanish genius's sentimental mood seems too cloying, but it never errs into kitsch: the subject of its deep humanism is not some wistful ideal, but an ordinary man of flesh and blood. Though the mood is lofty, within the figures flickers the ghost of Caravaggio's plebeian characters. One former critic characterized his art as "noble naturalism". The dignity of the characters derives primarily from sincere humility, and it is this virtue that characterizes the gesture of the donor of *Jesus Distributing Bread*, Canon Justino de Neve, who had his portrait placed among the needy pleading for charity.

Axel Vécsey

Guido Reni

(1575–1642)

The Crucifixion of Saint Peter, 1604

Pen and ink, wash over red chalk, 23 × 13.7 cm

Esterházy collection, purchased in 1871

2366

In the final decades of the sixteenth century a bustling artistic life developed in Bologna. Denijs Calvaert was the first to open a workshop there, to be followed shortly by the academy of the Carracci brothers, goaded on by the Fleming's success. The Carracci school, where the training centred on drawing from live models, soon enjoyed unparalleled popularity, and won over even Calvaert's best pupils. Guido Reni was the most talented of them, and with time his fame exceeded even that of his masters. Like many of his contemporaries, the young Reni also tried his fortune in Rome, where he was taken under the wing of Giuseppe Cesari, the favourite painter of Pope Clement VIII. It may have been Cesari's intercession that earned Reni the commission for the altarpiece of the church of San Paolo alle Tre Fontane in 1604. If contemporary gossip can be believed, Guido was a godsend to Cesari, enabling him to pluck the commission from the hand of his former apprentice and rival Caravaggio. The altarpiece representing the martyrdom of Saint Peter (now in the Pinacoteca Vaticana in Rome) reveals that Reni was truly at home in Caravaggio's 'hunted and dark manner'. Yet the raw naturalism based on sharp contrasts of light and shadow is counterbalanced by elegance, classical harmony and the accurate anatomy gleaned in the Carracci academy. The only surviving sketch for the altarpiece is our exceptionally vigorous sheet, which however faithfully evokes the dramatic power of its Caravaggiesque realism.

Zoltán Kárpáti

Guercino

(1591–1666)
The Flagellation of Christ, 1644
Oil on canvas, 351 × 176.5 cm
Bequest of János Pálffy, 1912
4225

Giovanni Francesco Barbieri eked out his first fifty years in his native town, day after day waiting for the death of his hated rival Guido Reni. Barbieri's squint, which earned him the moniker Guercino, was not his only fault: his contemporaries found him vulgar, frustrated, and coarse. So in vain was his talent recognized, he gained far fewer clients than his handsome and pleasantly mannered adversary, and jealousy poisoned his soul. But when in 1642 news came of his enemy's death, he immediately moved to Bologna to stake his claim to the vacant throne of the preeminent painter. The move was successful, Guercino soon earned fame, stacked up quite a fortune, and by all accounts even his manners improved.

By the time the opportunity arose, Guercino's painting style had grown to resemble that of his rival. The dark tone, unbridled motion and aggressive naturalism of his youthful works had given way to the complete opposite. In their place were the Raphael-inspired sunshine, clarity and temperance, with which 'the divine Guido' had endeared himself to the world. Nowhere is this as clear as in this enormous altarpiece, which was consecrated in August 1644, two years after Reni's death, in a private chapel of a family in Vicenza. Certain details copy slavishly one of Reni's last unfinished works with the same subject. But Guercino's Christ is more dignified, and rather than collapsing under the suffering, holds his head high to declare his triumph over those torturing him.

Axel Vécsey

Salomon van Ruysdael
(1600/02–1670)
After the Rain, 1631
Oil on panel, 56 × 86.4 cm
Esterházy collection, purchased in 1871
260

When Hendrick Goltzius made a few drawings of the coastal dunes near Haarlem in 1603, perhaps even he did not suspect he was starting a revolution in European landscape painting. Instead of the Italianate golden-age idylls, to the Haarlem masters it was the here-and-now that mattered, and they painted everyday Dutch flatlands: dunes, canals, village streets, and the sea. These had hitherto been considered unworthy as subjects for a picture, but now seemed appropriate for conveying the new idea of the nation. And to make the new relationship clear, the viewpoint was brought down from on high to the ground. Now the sky dominated the picture, and the moist air cast a veil over the landscape. The Haarlem landscapists are admired chiefly for their masterful suggestion of this humid atmosphere. Each artist was able to create a different mood. Of the two greatest masters it is said that in Jan van Goyen's works it always seems that rain is in the offing, while in Salomon van Ruysdael's we sense a fresh breeze has just dispersed the shower. In *After the Rain*, known by this title since the nineteenth century, one can almost smell the refreshing scent as the ground breathes after the storm. The crisp, crystal-clear outlines suggest that for a moment the mist has risen. The cool tones of colour create a chill mood, though a strip of the dune is bathed in golden radiance by the sun breaking through the clouds. In the house at the edge of the village the tired travellers find solace at last.

Axel Vécsey

Rembrandt van Rijn

(1606–1669)

Woman with a Child Frightened by a Dog, 1635–36

Pen and ink on paper, 18.2 × 14.5 cm

Esterházy collection, purchased in 1871

1589

Rembrandt is the key figure of seventeenth-century Dutch art, and one of the greatest engravers and drawers of all time. He had four children from his wife Saskia van Uylenburgh, who met an early death; only the youngest of them, Titus, lived to adulthood. In the first years of his marriage Rembrandt was keenly preoccupied with the depiction of women and children: one extant inventory of his goods lists one hundred and thirty-five such drawings. As well as his household, he liked to portray others too, and captured scenes from everyday life in lightning sketches, which did not necessarily serve any other purpose beyond the artist's observation.

In this drawing he brings a charming street scene to life. On the way home from the market a mother comforts her child, frightened by a dog: she kneels by him, embraces him protectively and smiles as she pacifies him. In the Frits Lugt collection in Paris there is a drawing in which the artist (probably still at the scene) put the three figures on paper. In the Budapest sheet Rembrandt elaborated the spontaneous sketch into a genre drawing: the group of figures is tighter-knit, their movements more clarified, and as he conjured up the surroundings, with a few brisk pen-strokes he sketched the steps and the house, with the caricature-like woman looking with curiosity from the window. This version was presumably made in the studio, and yet preserves the nimbleness of the sketches made from life.

Eszter Seres

Pieter Jansz. Saenredam
(1597–1665)
The Interior of Nieuwe Kerk in Haarlem, 1653
Oil on oak, 86 × 103 cm
Esterházy collection, purchased in 1871
311

A few decades ago the art history world was buzzing with a provocative theory put forward by an American scholar. According to this still hotly disputed thesis, Dutch art, unlike the Italian tradition, which always told stories, basically strove to observe and describe objects, and ultimately to know the world through experience; one might say this approach was of scientific nature, rather than literary. Whatever one's view of such a generalization, one thing is certain: a memorial statue to such an artistic attitude could be modelled on Saenredam. He developed a complex working method based on mechanical calculations so that he could depict with documentary fidelity the Protestant churches and town-hall chambers which symbolized the ideals of the young Dutch nation. His paintings were created through long months of painstaking work, and thus are extremely rare precious, with no more than sixty of them known. But art is never purely documentation, and sure enough not even Saenredam was always perfectly faithful to what he saw. Due to the carefully chosen viewpoints and light conditions, the spaces often appear (as in the present painting) lighter, airier, and more grandiose than the impression from a visit to the location itself. More surprising however is that this image of the Nieuwe Kerk includes several architectural elements which featured only in the plan, but for financial reasons were eventually not executed in the building.

Axel Vécsey

Jan Fijt

(1611–1661)

Still-life with Hare and Game Birds, c. 1642–50

Oil on canvas, 62.5 × 86 cm

Esterházy collection, purchased in 1871

729

Hunting has long been entertainment for the privileged. No wonder then that the genre of painted hunting trophies flourished most in Flanders in Rubens's time, which more than any other era was in the sway of the cult of heaving plenty and worldly extravagance. Surprisingly, though obviously not coincidentally, in the other half of the Netherlands, newly seceded Protestant Holland, an art of the most puritan approach sprang up simultaneously. One might think there would be no exchange between these two worlds, even though their watchful eyes were always fixed on the other – but there, indeed, was. The prince of game pieces, Jan Fijt visited Holland in 1642, after which the tone of his painting changed considerably. Into the triumphant uproar of brazen Baroque there crept more muted, melancholy chords. The magnificent spread of the kill of game here is more a lament to mortality, than an invitation to a vain banquet. The message is completed with a symbol aptly Dutch in its directness: thorns referring to the passion of Christ. But Fijt could not change his spots, and even with its serious content, in this picture the sound of triumph dominates – that of the painter, ostentatiously flaunting his truly compelling skill. And that of his virtuoso brush, which like Proust's famous madeleine, through the eye awakens the other senses too, so that the softness of the splendid hare's fur becomes almost palpable, or we strain to hear the dying warbles of these brilliantly coloured songbirds.

Axel Vécsey

Claude Lorrain

(1604/05–1682)
Villa in the Roman Campagna, c. 1646–47
Oil on canvas, 68.8 × 91 cm
Esterházy collection, purchased in 1871
708

Deerhunting, c. 1645
Pen-and-ink and wash over chalk, 23.3 × 32.9 cm
Esterházy collection, purchased in 1871
2849

The life of Claude Lorrain was like a fairytale. He was just twelve when after he set off from his native village in France all the way to Rome. With no experience but a brief apprenticeship in a pastry-cook's at home, there were gaps in his education, to say the least, and he never learnt Italian properly; yet the fashionable, urbane aristocracy adored him, and his pictures were so admired that there was a considerable business forging them. In spite of being a reserved dreamer he attained unparalleled success in the capital of intrigue and envy. He tamed even the archfoe of glory, time: the greatest landscapists of the nineteenth century – the British Turner, or the Hungarian Markó, still chased Claude's mellow sunlight.

For this is the secret of Claude's art: sunlight which permeates all and gives life. Whether he paints imaginary antique harbours, or the Campagna, the plains surrounding Rome, it is the light which clothes the view in the radiance of the Golden Age, and lends a cosmic dimension to modest settings. It seems as though Virgil's ancient idylls have come to life, though the Renaissance castles dominating the area are much more recent. The castle in this drawing is the famous La Crescenza, which often features in Claude's pictures, and following his example later artists (such as Corot) were also fond of painting it. Some believe the painting shows the same castle too, but this building, though assembled from familiar elements, is a product of the imagination.

Axel Vécsey

PREDIKER,
KOHELETH

Jan van der Heyden

(1637–1712)
Corner of a Room with Curios, 1712
Oil on canvas, 43 × 35.8 cm
Esterházy collection, purchased in 1871
201

The Bible in the foreground is open at the famous line from Ecclesiastes: *Vanity of vanities, all is vanity.* As if a stern lecturer were explaining with a cane in his hand, the book seems to force the message upon us: all earthly knowledge and beauty are futile, for in the end comes death, and all that man has accumulated vanishes.
Such 'vanitas still-lifes' have a long tradition, though initially they condemned only revelry. Here however the objects represent the entire worldly culture, not just the opulent but also the noble. We set out from Willem Blaeu's atlas, the origin of every Dutch expedition, which lies open where the country was 'born': the first victory of the war of independence was won at Bergen. Then we are taken on a journey over all the routes of the glorious Dutch merchant fleets, with a Turkish carpet, Chinese silk and porcelain, Japanese weapons and a stuffed armadillo from South America. Nor is classical culture, the cradle of European civilization, absent: above the fireplace is the tragedy of Dido, and the German cabinet is decorated with an image of Minerva. Finally, terrestrial and celestial globes raise the ensemble to the universal dimension. Van der Heyden painted this summative masterpiece at the age of seventy-five, the year he died, and the concept is obviously linked to the sense of the end drawing near. Though he may have felt it vanity, he did after all make a final display of the virtuoso skill which has protected his name from oblivion ever since.

Axel Vécsey

Bernardo Bellotto
(1721–1780)
View of Florence with the Arno, 1742
Oil on canvas, 62 × 90 cm
Esterházy collection, purchased in 1871
647

By the end of the eighteenth century Venice was living from its past glories. The main source of income in the city had become tourism, and where two centuries ago the crews of victorious fleets of ships had marched, now adventurers, courtesans and card-sharps teemed around the British, German and Hungarian gallants. Tourism gave birth to a new genre of painting: the cityscape, which the visitor could take home as a souvenir, there to conjure up the world of Casanova and Vivaldi.

The master who created the genre was Antonio Canale, known as Canaletto, though his nephew Bernardo Bellotto by no means fell short of him in quality. Yet while the uncle incessantly painted the familiar corners of Venice (a decade in London aside), Bellotto became a chronicler of the whole of Europe, from Rome to Vienna, from Dresden to Warsaw. Yet, albeit made in Florence, this enthralling youthful masterpiece cannot help but reveal where the artist learnt to look and to see. The precisely constructed lines of the buildings claim that we have here a document of photographic fidelity, yet the River Arno seems to don the mask of the Grand Canal in Venice. The more thickset forms of Florentine architecture are delicately, almost imperceptibly elongated, and the boats seem to wilfully imitate gondolas. By far the most noticeable give-away is the magical light sparkling on the surface of the water: perhaps it does indeed sparkle this way in Florence too, but only in Venice can it be observed so closely.

Axel Vécsey

Giovanni Battista Tiepolo

(1696–1770)
Vision of Saint James in the Battle of Clavijo, 1749–50
Oil on canvas, 317 × 163 cm
Esterházy collection, purchased in 1871
649

"It is as if God created Tiepolo for us. He follows in Veronese's path, all spirit, fire ablaze, his colours are marvellous, his speed astonishing," gushed the Swedish ambassador from Venice. Although the Stockholm job came to naught, Tiepolo was sought after by every court in Europe, and he produced legions of masterpieces from Madrid to Würzburg. His monumental picture of Saint James of Compostela was also made for an international commission. Ricardo Wall, Spanish ambassador to London (who later, despite being Irish, became prime minister), intended it for the altar of the embassy chapel. In the capital of Protestant England the Roman rite could be practised only in chapels of Catholic embassies, which thus became public spaces, displays of the power of these nations. The metaphor for Hispania's historic mission, the triumphant Battle of Clavijo in 844, seemed the perfect choice of subject for the location: the nation's patron saint appears as a vision to lead the Christians to victory against the pagans. Once finished, the painting was celebrated at a public exhibition in San Marco in Venice, and Tiepolo's son reproduced prints of it. (The head study was made for the engraving). Yet it was not, finally, installed in its intended place: the Spanish turned shy at the sight of the enormous battlehorse dominating most of the picture, which when placed on an altar would, they opined, provide fodder for the Protestants' accusations of idolatry in the Catholic veneration of images.

Axel Vécsey

Giovanni Domenico Tiepolo

(1727–1804)
Saint James, 1749–50
Red and white pastel on paper, 32.2 × 25.3 cm
Gift of Simon Meller, 1929
1929–2164

Franz Xaver Messerschmidt
(1736–1783)
Character Head: The Gentle, Quiet Sleep, 1777–83
Tin, 43 × 26 × 22 cm
Bequest of Jenő Zichy, 1906
53.656

Character Head: Childish Weeping, 1771–83
Tin and lead alloy, 44 × 27 × 22 cm
Purchased in Vienna, 1894
51.936

Character Head: The Yawner, 1771–81
Tin, 42 × 21 × 20 cm
Bequest of Jenő Zichy, 1906
53.655

The upward path of Messerschmidt's career was brought to a halt by a mysterious illness. He was tipped to be professor of sculpture in the Academy of Arts in Vienna, and was a favourite sculptor in the imperial court, when he was suddenly pensioned off on account of his mental illness. Upset, he took leave of Vienna for good and settled in Pozsony. It was here that most of his *Character heads* were made, a unique series of about fifty busts. Much head-scratching has gone on over the interpretation of the busts, which after the sculptor's death were displayed as a raree-show in the Prater in Vienna. Initially they were associated with the artist's presumed schizophrenia, and in a Freudian vein they were seen as a reflection of the subconscious. Others suggested that the heads were inspired by the peculiar methods of the doctor Franz Anton Mesmer, a close friend of the artist's, which are held to be the forerunner of psychotherapy. Mesmer believed the root of psychological and even indirectly physical diseases was the disorder of the magnetic field of the nervous system. During the sessions Messerschmidt would have seen such extreme emotions on the patients' faces. It is true, however, that in Messerschmidt's time the representation of human emotions was a central issue of art. As a teacher at the academy he certainly knew contemporary studies of expressions, thus in spite of their traditional titles the heads explore various, sometimes extreme grimaces rather than human characters.

Miriam Szőcs

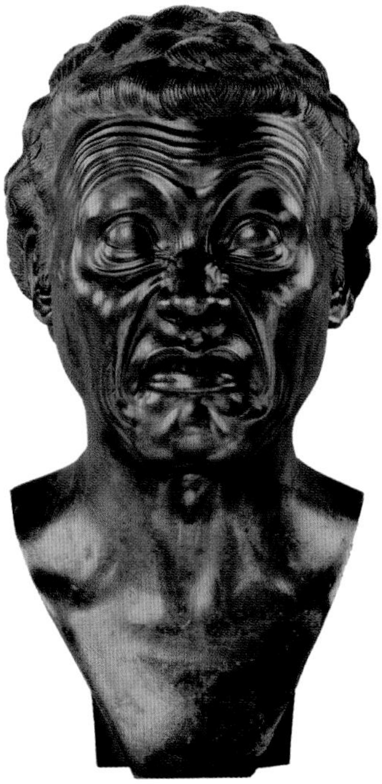

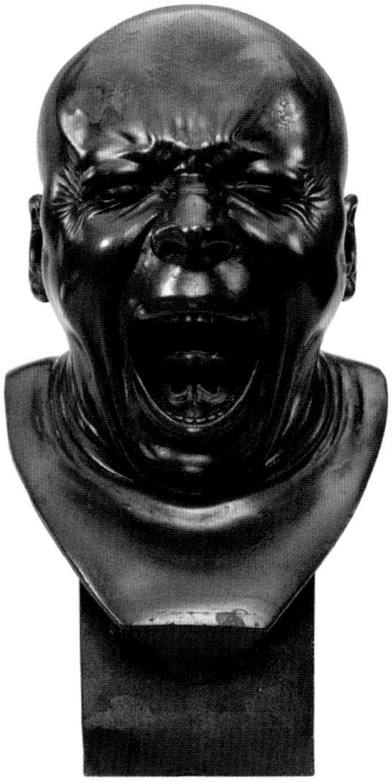

Francisco de Goya

(1746–1828)
Water-carrier, c. 1808–12
Oil on canvas, 68 × 52 cm
Esterházy collection, purchased in 1871
760

Whether Goya was the last great old master or the first modern genius is a spurious dilemma: he did not straddle the border between two eras – he himself was the border. Once he was celebrated for his carefree Rococo palace decorations and grandiose portraits; the Goya admired today is rather the one who opened Pandora's box, and for the first time set free the inner demons of the human soul and the horrors of war.

The *Water-carrier* bears the imprint of both Goyas. At first glance it seems a simple rustic genre picture: a somewhat rough-hewn, yet ethereally charming young girl carries water and food to someone. A forerunner to this figure can be found on tapestry designs twenty years earlier, which Goya made for the Madrid court, at a moment of European optimism, when it seemed that the Enlightenment would bring general welfare. But then all hell was breaking loose and by the time the picture was made Spain had been sacked by Napoleon's troops. The idyllic world of the tapestries had gone, and the air is charged with a surly restlessness instead. Indeed, it is war we see here: the water is needed by the nameless heroes of Zaragoza, who held up the invaders practically with their bare hands. It is not suffering that dominates here, as in the famous *Disasters of War* prints. With a pathos unusual for Goya, the figure of the girl is ennobled almost to the status of a memorial: a statue to the stubborn, ordinary heroism of a people seeking to set the world back on the right track.

Axel Vécsey

Eugène Delacroix

(1798–1863)

Horse Startled by Lightning, c. 1825–29

Watercolour, whitewash 23.6 × 32 cm

Gift of Pál Majovszky, 1934

1935–2698

Delacroix's art embodied all that was important in Romanticism. Breaking with classicism's strict cult of line, he built his paintings primarily upon the expressive power of colours, while he often turned to Baroque art for inspiration. He was attracted by unusual, exotic subjects, imaginary depictions of hunts, and grandiose historic scenes. Like most of his contemporaries Delacroix too was enthusiastic about the Greek War of Independence: one of his most famous works, the *Massacre at Chios* pays tribute to the victims of the Ottoman slaughter.

While preparing for this monumental painting he was confronted with the problem of the anatomical representation of the horse. Though he persevered in studying the motions of horses, his contemporaries and predecessors also exercised a considerable influence on him. His horses derive just as much from Géricault's Romantic paintings, and the Parthenon frieze he had admired on his brief trip to London, as to the British sporting painters who specialized in the portrayal of horses and dogs.

The horse in this splendid watercolour, rearing up startled by lightning, is borrowed from a painting by the English painter Sawrey Gilpin, reworked with Romantic imagination into an enigmatic creation of dramatic zeal. Delacroix held it in special esteem, so much that though he was usually reluctant to part from his drawings, he did give this one to a friend, the portrait painter and landscapist Louis-August Schwiter shortly after its execution.

Zoltán Kárpáti

Gustave Courbet

(1819–1877)
Wrestlers, 1853
Oil on canvas, 252 × 198 cm
From the collection of Ferenc Hatvany, 1951
502.B

At the centre of Courbet's life was the struggle for his artistic ideals and his political views. A great master of realist painting, he placed this battle at the focus of *Wrestlers.* The scene is set in Paris, at the racegrounds behind the Arc de Triomphe. In the foreground is a heated battle between the athletes, yet their forms give a sense of immobility and rigidity. Rather than motion, Courbet places the emphasis on the anatomical detail of strong but strained bodies, highlighting the tense muscles and swollen veins. The stands behind them are occupied by genteel onlookers – but it is strikingly apparent that the contest is for the benefit of the viewer, rather than the barely visible audience. The restoration in 2009 revived Courbet's vivid colours, thus making the difference in style (colours, proportions and brushwork alike) between the background and the protagonists in the foreground even more apparent. The difference derives partly from Courbet's working method (figures were developed in the workshop and their environment was usually painted more freely) but also reveals that he wanted to draw attention not to the entertainments of the Parisian bourgeoisie but to the suffering, struggling masses. This political overtone refers to the social difficulties of the years following the rise to power of Napoleon III. Yet it was not this, but its full-blooded realism that prompted most critics at the 1853 Paris salon to condemn the work.

Zsófia Kovács

Honoré Daumier

(1808–1879)
Circus Criers, 1864–65
Red and black chalk, and wash on paper, 39.8 × 30.4 cm
Hatvany collection, purchased in 1950
1950–4276

The greatest caricaturist of the nineteenth century, Honoré Daumier was born into a poor family in Marseille, and all his life he felt a close bond with the outcasts of society. The political satires made for daily papers and anti-monarchist satirical rags, which made him famous, were often banned, then after King Louis Philippe reintroduced censorship the artist was condemned to jail. Daumier's interest was compulsively drawn towards everyday subjects. Though his mockery of the absurdities of his time was no less biting, he never lost his empathy. He published more than five thousand lithographs, in addition to making countless paintings and drawings, highly respected by collectors. Daumier was constantly occupied by the world of the theatre and circus. At the edge of society, not only were these showfolk living by their own laws a favourite subject for art, but with time they became a symbol of artistic freedom. In the 1860s Daumier dedicated a whole series of drawings and graphics to acrobats, wrestlers, and clowns. Around 1864 he made a loosely connected series of drawings on circus criers, who with their stentorian voices and general hullaballoo invite the public to the show. This highly expressive sketch well illustrates Daumier's brilliant drawing skill. This composition, sketched with a relaxed but sure hand, shows the distorted face and grotesque posture of the figures, though their gestures have been repeatedly altered.

Eszter Seres

Edouard Manet
(1832–1883)
Lady with a Fan (Jeanne Duval), 1862
Oil on canvas, 90 × 113 cm
Purchased in Berlin, 1916
368.B

Charles Baudelaire, the extraordinary poet who trod the path between Romanticism and Symbolism, met the mulatto actress Jeanne Duval in 1842. "Sorceress with the ebony thighs, child of black midnights," he apostrophized her in one of his finest poems. Their liaison lasted a good ten years, but Baudelaire continued to support Duval, who was paralysed in one leg. Manet painted this "Black Venus" in 1862, at the peak of his career as a painter. The composition of the picture is not linked to prototypes, and Manet designed it masterfully. The canvas is dominated by the enormous crinoline, striped white on white, which seems to have a life of its own. The right hand resting on the curved sofa is counterpoised by the foot peeping out from under the skirt, whose emphatic positioning may refer to the tragic illness. The enchanting lace curtain in the background appears as though an arched proscenium around the haggard face of the fated, sick actress. Curator Simon Meller pointed out already in his proposal for the painting's acquisition that this work of unique beauty came close in terms of colouring to some Spanish old masters. At the same time the sketchy brushwork of this recently restored work, and its buoyant energy reflect the new style Manet adopted afterwards his Spanish period.

Judit Geskó

Pierre-Auguste Renoir

(1841–1919)
Boating, 1885–86
Watercolour on paper, 30.4 × 47.5 cm
Gift of Pál Majovszky, 1935
1935–2762

Like many Impressionist painters, Renoir's career was slow getting off the ground. Since the Paris Salon persistently rejected his paintings, he joined the group of Impressionists led by Monet. Though he is considered a founder of the movement, he was more closely bound to traditional subjects than his fellow Impressionists. He greatly admired the art of Raphael and Ingres, and following in their footsteps he was preoccupied with figurative art. He also transferred the experience of *plein air* painting into his studio compositions, with consummate skill. The protagonists of his pictures, with their vibrant luminosity and shot colours, are almost always human figures; one of his favourite recurrent subjects was the female nude.

During the 1870s and '80s Renoir was fond of representing merry companies rowing up and down the Seine. In his boating works the features of his model and later wife Aline Charigot, can often be identified. Renoir spent July 1886 in La Roche-Guyon on the banks of the Seine. The Budapest watercolour captures a moment from this summer, and in a typically Impressionist style the painter suggests the surroundings with easy brushstrokes and diaphanous colours. As well as the main scene, the artist drew the figures' faces elsewhere too: while the man's features are sketched with delicate brushstrokes, Aline's face is worked out in detail on the far right.

Eszter Seres

Auguste Rodin
(1840–1917)
Eternal Spring, 1901
Carrarra marble, 75 × 81 × 44 cm
Purchased from the artist, 1901
3394.U

Auguste Rodin, the most influential master of modern sculpture, received a commission in 1880 for the main entrance of the planned new Musée des Arts Décoratifs. He decided to decorate the door wings with bronze reliefs with scenes from Dante's *Inferno*. *The Gates of Hell* had a long protracted period of gestation, but the grandiose plan was never realized. The sketches, however, provided countless ideas for other sculptures, including some of his best-known works. *Eternal Spring* was born of the reworking of just such a detail, a metamorphosis bringing to life smoothly polished forms as they slowly disengage from the block of raw marble and assume the figures of two people. At the centre of Rodin's universe was the woman as an inspiring muse, the source and destiny of everything. Many of his themes are pregnant with passionate desire or unbridled sexuality, but more than anything he was preoccupied with the beauty of the human body. In the Paris World's Fair of 1900 the celebrated master set up his own private pavilion to display his works. It was here the plaster parts of *The Gates of Hell* as well as the independent statues derived from the project went on public display for the first time. Gábor Térey, chief curator of the Budapest Museum of Fine Arts, was deeply impressed by this show, and visited Rodin personally to order works for the museum. This marble *Eternal Spring* was made upon this commission, and he also bought four other bronze and plaster sculptures from the artist.

Ferenc Tóth

Claude Monet

(1840–1926)
Three Fishing Boats, 1885
Oil on canvas, 73 × 92.5 cm
Purchased in 1945
436.B

Claude Monet was perhaps the most respected member of the group of Impressionists. At various phases of his life he often spent time on the Normandy coast, which was one of his favourite subjects. One such fondly frequented place was Étretat, a small fishing village and weekend resort close to Le Havre. He regularly painted on the shore, and with a lust for adventure set about discovering an almost unapproachable stretch of coast to the west. Even in the harshest of circumstances he would be outside, capturing the landscape, the movement of ships, or perhaps the herring fishing boats pulled up onto the pebbly beach. We see these latter slightly from above, and this bold view narrows the space, rendering the composition tenser. For Monet the key issue was to suggest the frothy waves of the sea and the currents of air, for which he uses broad, bouyant brushtrokes.

Monet's coastal paintings mostly depict deserted, unpeopled places, and there is nothing to show that at the time Étretat was a popular resort. He was interested not in anecdotal episodes, but in effects of form and colour. The writer Guy de Maupassant, who at the time was also staying in Étretat and often met Monet, described his friend's working method, as he took five or six canvases with him which he swapped around according to the changing light. When Monet returned home to Giverny in December, he took with him more than fifty half-finished works, which he later finished in his studio.

Ferenc Tóth

Paul Cézanne
(1839–1906)
A Buffet, 1874–77
Oil on canvas, 65.5 × 81 cm
Gift of Baron Ferenc Hatvany, 1917
371.B

Cézanne spent most of his life in the town where he was born, Aix-en-Provence. The Budapest still-life was made in the coastal town of Estaque near Aix and Marseille, where Cézanne moved several times.

When the picture was painted in the mid-1870s Cézanne was friends with the most important Impressionist painters: Pissarro, Monet and Renoir. At this time, the palette of his earlier so-called Baroque-style paintings gave way to lighter colours, but rather than the Impressionists' method of painting he was preoccupied with capturing what is lasting and permanent. He regularly studied works in museums, plaster cast collections, and reproductions in art journals. Just as the poetry of Charles Baudelaire can be viewed as the culmination of previous movements, so can Cézanne's still-lifes from the 1870s, for which he studied the compositions of Chardin and seventeenth-century Spanish still-life painters. Cézanne used what he learnt from still-lifes in his portraits and landscapes too.

The still-lifes make up a considerable part of his oeuvre, and several of them were expressions of the artist's momentary state of mind. The Budapest still-life expresses symmetry in asymmetry. The top and the shelf of the buffet are linked by a full bottle of wine, as a solid point between the fragile white porcelain cups, the wine-glass, the rumpled white tea-cloth and the mound of feather-light ladyfingers.

Judit Geskó

Vincent van Gogh

(1853–1890)
The Parsonage Garden at Nuenen in Winter, 1884
Pen and brown ink, whitewash, 51.5 × 38 cm
Gift of Pál Majovszky, 1934
1935–2785

Van Gogh was nearing thirty when he finally decided to be a painter. His resolution was preceded by a decade of soul-searching and struggling. He had worked as an art dealer, then following his father's example had served as a priest. His superiors sent him to minister to the coal miners in Borinage, where he spent his time teaching the destitute at the edge of society, caring for them and preaching to them. It was a bitter blow to him when his contract was not renewed. Most likely this too contributed to his taking up painting, at the instigation of his brother Theo.
In December 1883 he arrived in the parish in Nuenen to spend the next two years living with his parents. Although he had already regularly engaged in drawing, he now determined to study. Following the 'academic' curriculum he devised for himself, in the first year he concentrated solely on the study of drawing. The parsonage garden was particularly dear to his heart, and in early spring he made many drawings of it. Later two sheets of a series of six large-scale landscapes were also dedicated to this subject. One of these is this early masterpiece of Van Gogh's. The gnarled trunks of the bare trees dominate a barren landscape captured with dramatic power: a poetic document of the inner solitude of the artist working in seclusion. Van Gogh was well aware that this series was somewhat special, so he sent a few sheets to his art-dealer brother to sell. His expectations were, however, as so often, to meet with disappointment.

Zoltán Kárpáti

Paul Gauguin
(1848–1903)
Black Pigs, 1891
Oil on canvas, 91 × 72 cm
Purchased in 1913
355.B

As a successful stockbroker Gauguin initially dabbled in painting only as a hobby. But in 1883, prompted by Pissarro, he broke with his original profession for good to dedicate his life to painting. With his first pictures he regularly featured in the group exhibitions of the Impressionists. Leaving behind the European illusionist traditions, he increasingly sought stimulation in exotic and primitive cultures. He found family ties depressing, felt disenchanted with civilization, and fled further and further from them. First to Pont Aven in Brittany, then to Martinique, and finally in 1891 to Tahiti.

The art of Gauguin became consummate in his years in Tahiti. He sought to express in the language of painting the dignity and harmony these peoples had retained from their ancient way of life and culture. The *Black Pigs*, which he painted in his first year in Tahiti, captures an exciting moment of stylistic transition. The foliage of the trees and the reed roof of the hut are formed in the Impressionist fashion with iridescent parallel brushstrokes, but these are gradually replaced by more uniform surfaces of colour, and the forms are outlined with strong blue lines. Here, particularly in the case of the animals and the female figures depicted in a state of archaic rest, he used compact, simplified forms. Within the deliberately composed structure the spatial relations of the motifs is governed by formal unity.

Ferenc Tóth

Henri de Toulouse-Lautrec
(1864–1901)
The Ladies in the Dining Room, 1895
Oil on cardboard, 61 × 81 cm
Purchased in 1913
356.B

Writers of the last third of the nineteenth century such as Zola and Maupassant were keen on taking as their subjects the oppressed fate of people living on the edge of society. Though of aristocratic lineage, due to a childhood accident which stunted his growth, Toulouse-Lautrec often felt shut out himself from the fashionable world of healthy people. He found his favourite models in the world lying beyond the reach of morality, in the nights of fin-de-siècle Paris. As well as the smoky dens of Montmartre, and its danseuses, enveloped in curious mystery, he captured the everyday life of prostitutes with irony and deep empathy, even dignifying it. Many of his pictures are set in the brothel in Rue des Moulins, which opened in 1895. Thanks to the typical gestures and expressive faces, recorded with sharp psychological observation, some resident cocottes can be recognized on several pictures. Some of the exaggeratingly presented 'ladies' here are also known by name. The fourth member of the company at table can be seen only in the mirror: this daring composition relates to the snap takes of photography. The fast, sketch-like brushstrokes in several places left the board's own colour exposed, and with its raw materiality and warm tone it fits integrally in the composition's atmosphere. The dynamic painting technique, the silhouettes shaded reservedly with colour, and the laconic directness of the way he captures the environment conjure up the mood of Lautrec's Art Nouveau posters.

Ferenc Tóth

Pablo Picasso
(1881–1973)
Mother and Child, 1905
Watercolour on paper, 35.3 × 25.3 cm
Gift of Ferenc Hatvany, 1918
1918–461

The year 1906 marked the end of Picasso's first distinct period, which because of the predominant colour and its melancholy mood is called the 'blue period'. A recurrent theme of these works, as well as the outcasts, the poor, beggars, and cripples, was the circus, something he enthused about all his life. In the sunnier works of the following 'rose period' in place of the cold blues and greys we now find warmer pinks, oranges and pale reds. The former guant rendering of human relationships gave way to a more emotional characterization.

This watercolour of a mother and child signals the turning-point in Picasso's career. It was made one year after the artist settled permanently in Paris. Here he worked in a modest studio flat, in the neighborhood of poets and painters, where new friendships and loves were born. One of the latter was the model for many of his works, Fernande Olivier, whom he portrayed on the reverse of this sheet. The *Mother and Child* is one of the very first works of the rose period, and is still closely linked to the previous style. Picasso isolated the figures from a composition he also engraved, representing a family of acrobats. The self-contained group of mother and child seems to melt into the dark background, thus enhancing the sense of solitude and haggardness. Alongside the severe colours, Picasso used patches of red to enliven the work, which is lent a touch of lyricism by the sensitive outline of the mother's face and the tender gestures.

Eszter Seres

Oskar Kokoschka
(1886–1980)
Veronica's Veil, 1911
Oil on canvas, 119 × 80 cm
Purchased in Budapest, 1964
542.B

Also known as a poet and dramatist, Oskar Kokoschka was a pupil of one of the most famous figures of the Secession, Gustav Klimt. In contrast to earlier traditions, Kokoschka sought not a naturalistic representation of reality, but the psychological exploration of the inner self. His dramatic portraits, which focused on the mapping of the soul, made him one of the authorities of German Expressionism. *Veronica's Veil* is both his first sacred painting and also one of the key works of his early oeuvre, which he referred to as the "religious picture closest to my heart". Apocryphal sacred texts relate how Veronica, a woman of Jerusalem, with her shawl wiped the blood and sweat from Christ's face on the way to Calvary; this shawl then miraculously preserved the image of the Saviour's face. Her white-hot angular face radiates melancholy, and the gesture with which her long fingers gently and protectively embosoms the blood-soaked shawl can be traced back to the tradition of Madonnas nursing the Child, or lamenting the dead Christ. Her figure is bathed in a cone of light. The full moon behind, a symbol of femininity, hints at Alma Mahler, the widow of composer Gustav Mahler, with whom the painter had a brief but passionate love affair. But the idea of the picture can perhaps be derived from an even more profane episode in his life: according to Kokoschka's memoirs, when the picture was made, his atelier windows were being cleaned by the concierge's daughter Veronica.

Márton Orosz

Egon Schiele
(1890–1918)
Two Girls Embracing, 1915
Pencil, watercolour and gouache, 48.5 × 32.6 cm
Purchased in Vienna, 1915
1915–933

Although the activity of Sigmund Freud was for a long time a source of controversy, his teachings, which liberated the deepest strata of the human soul, found fertile ground in the artistic life of fin-de-siècle Vienna. The erotic drawings and nude photographs of Gustav Klimt, the leading figure of the Viennese Secession, opened the way to the uninhibited depiction of sexuality. The erotically overcharged atmosphere of the city is well illustrated by the fact that during his brief, barely ten-year career, Egon Schiele found buyers almost only for his erotic drawings. Schiele was only seventeen when he was introduced to Klimt, who recognized the talent of the younger man, and became one of his main supporters. Initially the relationship between the two artists was so close that Schiele eventually 'inherited' the older painter's lover. As well as Klimt's art, the liberating spirit of the exhibitions held in the Secession building, particularly the Van Gogh, Toulouse-Lautrec and Munch works shown here, exercised a great influence on the young artist. Even among his nudes, shown with no taboos, with embarrassing openness, and often in provocative poses, a special place is held by the sheets showing lesbian couples. The models in this extremely decorative pencil drawing coloured with aquarelle are given a dispassionate rendering which camouflages all emotion and lends a distinctly melancholy mood to the work.

Zoltán Kárpáti

Kurt Schwitters

(1887–1948)
Merz 50, 1922
Collage, paper, 22 × 16 cm
Purchased from Sándor Bortnyik, 1972
K.72.2

Dadaism, one of the most intriguing artistic movements of the twentieth century, was born in Zurich, home to many émigrés, and at the same time a string of artists working in New York, Berlin and Paris began working in a similar vein. Developing as a reaction to the war, this trend set itself against bourgeois values and artistic conventions, while it lauded irrationalism and intuition in place of reason and logic. Kurt Schwitters, after his application was rejected, was never formally a member of the movement, yet he became the most consistent proponent of Dadaist ideas. His *Merz* pictures and reliefs (the nonsensical word was taken from a fragment of the German word 'Kommerz,' or 'commerce') are mostly small collages of a wide variety of *objets trouvés*; a kind of 'trashcan poetry'. Schwitters used almost everything in them, from pieces of wood and iron lying in the street, through tattered rags, to used envelopes, shreds of newspaper, and tram tickets. His chief work, the *Merzbau* (Merz building), a monumental trash sculpture occupying two floors of his house in Hannover, was built over a period of a decade. This collage, number fifty, made of train tickets, chocolate wrappers, scraps of newspapers and rags, was given by Schwitters to Sándor Bortnyik, a Hungarian avant-garde artist, at the international Dadaist meeting in Weimar in autumn 1922. With a playful, genuine Dadaist gesture he labelled the work with a scrap from a sell-by date inscription of a box of cocoa: 'März/Ap'.

Zoltán Kárpáti

Simon Hantaï

(1922–2008)
Untitled, c. 1951–52
Oil on canvas, 105 × 145 cm
Purchased, 2008
2008.1.U

The Hungarian émigré Simon Hantaï (originally Hantai) settled in Paris in 1949. This painting was made some years later, in a particularly experimental, innovative phase of his early oeuvre, in which Hantaï experimented with various new techniques such as collage, frottage, scraping away the paint layer, or a method which became central to his later art: folding and crumpling the canvas. The energy of his artistic search is clear even in this work, rich as it is in new formal solutions.
The net structure visible in the upper part of the painting soon dissolves in the free flow of forms that covers the entire picture surface. The surface is a frenzy activity, showing a rich texture, and the river of paint dripped onto the canvas weaves its way across almost the whole surface. Between the greyish, brownish earth tones there appear more vivid patches, but they are not clearly recognizable forms, and thus offer the viewer countless possibilities for association.
Best characterized as a kind of "creative chaos", this painting is a cosmic vision, and conjures up the movements in the depths of the earth, or biological processes as seen under the microscope. When this work was painted Hantaï was probably not yet in direct contact with the Surrealists (André Breton, the main theorist behind Surrealism, wrote the introduction to Hantaï's exhibition in Paris in 1953), however the influence of the group is quite apparent in this liberated work, which also makes use of automatism.

Zsófia Kovács

Josef Albers
(1888–1976)
Light Grey Wall, 1958
Oil on canvas, 65.5 × 81.5 cm
Gift of Victor Vasarely, 1969
576.B

Josef Albers is one of the most important proponents of geometric abstraction, and his activity as an artist is inseparable from his influential work as a teacher. In the 1920s he taught in the Bauhaus, and after it was closed in prestigious American universities such as Black Mountain College, Harvard and Yale. He summarized his courses in colour theory in 1963 in his book *The Interaction of Color.*
The *Light Grey Wall* is closely related to Albers's theoretical research. It is a sequel to the *Adobe* series, the idea for which came to him in Mexico in 1947. This is a long line of colour variations, on a geometric pattern made of the same repeated horizontal and upright rectangles, like the puritan Mexican adobe houses. The interaction of colours and forms sets the apparently static composition into motion. The two 'windows' seem sometimes to approach, and then to recede. The planes and fields of colour open as a seemingly infinite deep space, then close like a solid wall. Though the glowing reds and cool deep blues are here replaced by various shades of grey, the image is just as intense as in the preceding series.
Albers considered his pictures to be objects of meditation, which challenge the manner of human perception, activate vision and 'open eyes'. This is well illustrated by the *Light Grey Wall*, which creates a playful teasing between the viewer's gaze and the picture surface. 'Art is not to be looked at; Art is looking at us,' as the artist wrote in his ars-poetica poem.

Dávid Fehér

Ilya Kabakov

(b. 1933)
The Fly, 1982
India ink, pen and colour pencil on paper, 63.3 × 44 cm
Purchased, 1989
K.89.1.

Ilya Kabakov is one of the defining underground artists of the period of Eastern European dictatorships. At their first open-air exhibition in Moscow in 1974, bulldozers crushed the works of the world-famous environment and installation artist. Kabakov and his friends in the 70s and 80s were not allowed to have an official exhibition in the Russian capital. However, in 1982–83, as part of an unusual artistic campaign, Kabakov organized a fictive exhibition entitled "Fly with Wings" in the virtual halls of the Pushkin Museum. Kabakov's Budapest series of drawings "The Fly" consists of a central drawing of a house fly and sixty textual panels. On the panels the artist has written sentences in India ink. In a rough-and-ready form he also drew up the plan for laying out all the sheets. The resulting installation model is partly a narrative work (since reading the texts the viewer becomes a part of several stories), and partly a concept work rich in association. The graphic elements are drastically simplified, and the central drawing and the sentences are full of artistic and philosophical references. Interestingly, the interpretation of the work has altered over the decades.

There was a form of freedom which the artists of Eastern Europe could enjoy: they could stand outside the world they lived in. This is what Kabakov's work represents.

Judit Geskó

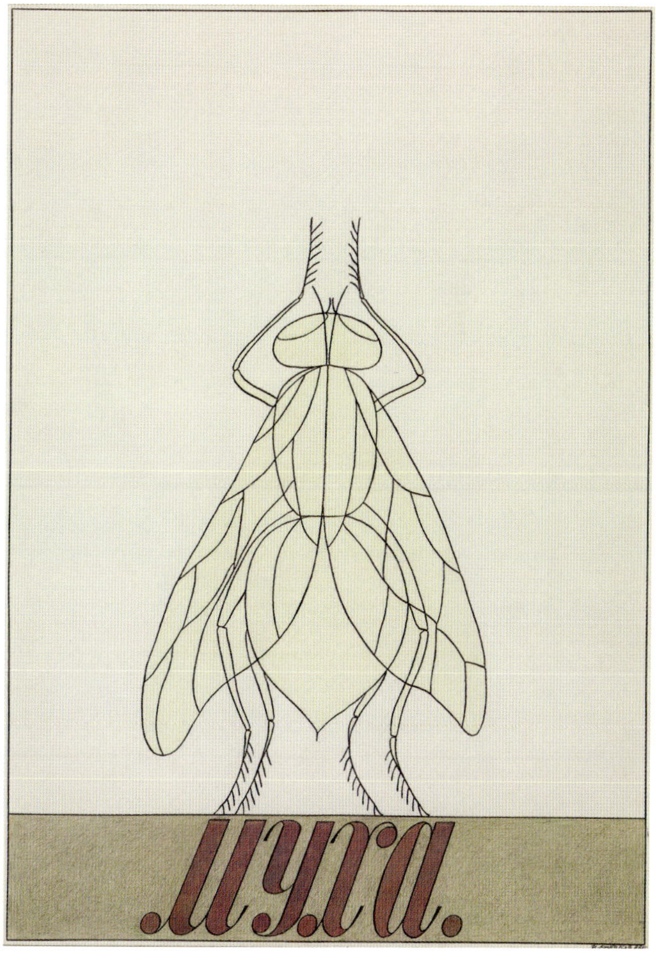

Anthony Caro
(b. 1924)
Catalan Song, 1987–1988
Steel, artificial rust coating, 114.5 × 73.5 × 33 cm
Purchased, 1994
94.1.U

Anthony Caro is a prominent figure in twentieth-century art, and one of the creators of modern British sculpture. In the 1950s he developed a sculptural language that drew on the achievements of Cubism, then from the end of the decade, leaving behind figurativeness, he began to build compositions freely developing in space from units welded together and painted one colour. These pieces of steel, cut to irregular shapes and exposing the texture of crude metal, lend an associative mood and a moving lyricism to Caro's sculptures. Evoking movement, and often playing on spatiality, on the ambiguity and interchangeability of inside and outside, in the artist's view these works lie halfway between architecture and sculpture, and come into their own when the viewer walks around them.

Catalan Song is from one of Caro's most poetic series. In 1987 he was invited to Barcelona to create works reflecting the colourful culture of the Mediterranean city at the sculpture workshop Casa de la Caritat. This sculpture (which he completed in his London studio) uses the characteristic forms of Gaudí's city, and the airily graceful wrought-iron ornamentation of Catalan Art Nouveau. Through a virtuoso interworking of the filigree-like elements (window gratings and other utilitarian objects) Caro created a rhythmically articulated, balanced sculpture, and he was able to accentuate the elegance of the piece by rustification of the surface with a rust coating.

Márton Orosz

Antoni Tàpies
(1923–2012)
Gothic Box, 1989
Chamotte clay, glaze, 18 × 23 × 38 cm
Purchased in 2009
2009.1.U

'For me any spontaneous gesture, if it expresses something human, even graffiti on a wall, is more valuable than entire museums full of painting which is not related to life,' wrote Antoni Tàpies, the recently deceased revolutionary figure of Catalan art. Barely legible, scribbled signs which preserve the spontaneity of touch are recurring motifs in his paintings, drawings and sculptures. The surface of the *Gothic Box* too is covered with various mysterious incised signs: wavy lines reminiscent of an archaic decorative pattern, and Tàpies's familiar cross motif, which has sacred connotations as well as referring to the artist's name. On another side is a twisting figure of eight like a Moebius strip, perhaps referring to infinity, invoking the spirit of Zen Buddhism. It is of course an open question whether these signs convey any symbolic meaning, or simply commemorate the act of leaving a mark.

The rough surface of the box bears the marks of firing in the kiln, and its patina seems to have formed over millennia. It looks like an archaeological find, and its palimpsest-like surface evokes the 'greyish, blackish, cracked walls' of Barcelona's admired Gothic quarter, where, as the artist says, 'the entire history of the country is written'. The ancient walls here belong to an unopenable solid unit hinting at an antique sepulchre or a medieval reliquary; with its invisible interior it addresses the relationship between art and emptiness, a recurrent issue in the work of Tàpies.

Dávid Fehér

Index

Publisher: **Dr. László Baán**
Production coordinator: **Krisztián Fonyódi**

Edited by **Axel Vécsey**
with assistance by **Zoltán Bartos**

Authors of the entries:
Dávid Fehér
Judit Geskó
Zoltán Kárpáti
Katalin Kóthay
Zsófia Kovács
Szilvia Lakatos
Éva Liptay
Márton Orosz
Manga Pattantyús
Eszter Seres
Miriam Szőcs
Ferenc Tóth
Axel Vécsey

English translation: **Richard Robinson**

Designers: **Eszter Balder, Dávid Remsey**
Photographers: **Dénes Józsa, Csanád Szesztay**
Printer: **Keskeny és Társai 2001 Ltd.**

On the cover: **Lucas Cranach the Elder: Salome with the Head of Saint John the Baptist,** 1530s (detail). Inv. no. 132 (see pp. 74–75)
On page 2: **Auguste Rodin: Eternal Spring,** 1901. Inv. no. 3394.U (see p. 127)
On page 147: **Workshop of Pietro Lombardo: Well-head from the Budapest palace of the Károlyi family,** Venice, late 15th century (detail). Inv. no. 57.6

First edition, 2013
ISBN: 978-615-5304-02-6

The publication was made possible by the generous support of MKB BANK